The Great Jackass Fallacy

The Great Jackass Fallacy

Harry Levinson
*Thomas Henry Carroll-Ford Foundation
Distinguished Visiting Professor of
Business Administration
Harvard University
1968–1972*

Division of Research
Graduate School of Business Administration
Harvard University
Boston · 1973

Library of Congress Catalog Card No. 72–92135
ISBN 0–87584–100–7

Printed in the United States of America

To Harry and Minnie Nudell,
my uncle and aunt, whose modesty and humble
life station belie the power and significance
of their affectionate inspiration and esteem.

Foreword

THERE IS nothing more central to management than the question of human motivation: Why do people strive to accomplish tasks, to lead others? During Professor Levinson's productive four years at the Harvard Business School, there was no issue of more concern to him. He struggled to understand better the assumptions about human motivation that underlay various management practices, and to persuade his colleagues and teach his students about the negative consequences of practices based on faulty assumptions.

The assumption that people are motivated by rewards and punishments, Professor Levinson calls "The Jackass Fallacy." He has detected this Fallacy as corrupting the techniques of management appraisal, as underlying the conflicts of family businesses, as contributing to the failures of mergers, and as causing a host of other seemingly unrelated problems for managers. He reported many of his observations in the form of articles published by the *Harvard Business Review* and other journals. Each article made an important point to managers, but they all also sounded a common theme. At our invitation, Professor Levinson has synthesized a number of these *Harvard Business Review* articles and added new material to create this volume and present before management an important and persuasive message.

Significant to the entirely new material written for this volume is the brief but emotionally powerful Chapter 11, which reflects upon his experience at the Harvard Business School. Here the author becomes the psychological man and shares his own feelings about the continuity of his efforts in the lives of others. In those few pages it is apparent that his experiences at the Business School, whatever frustrations they may also have included, were indeed gratifying to him.

Soldiers Field
Boston, Massachusetts
October 1972

RICHARD E. WALTON
Director of the
Division of Research

Preface

THE THOMAS HENRY CARROLL-FORD FOUNDATION professorship provides an opportunity for the incumbent to make a planned contribution to the work of the Harvard Business School of such a character as to have an impact on present or future research activities at the School and to further his own research and development interests. The professorship is a two-way contribution: to the work of the School and to the career of the holder.

In the four years (1968–1972) during which I was honored to hold this professorship, I was enabled to bring to fruition many of the tasks, ideas, and projects upon which I had been working for the previous twelve years. These included three books—*The Exceptional Executive* (Cambridge, Mass.: Harvard University Press, 1968); *Executive Stress* (New York: Harper & Row, 1970); and *Organizational Diagnosis* (Cambridge, Mass.: Harvard University Press, 1972)—and preliminary work on a fourth concerned with organizational intervention. In addition, the opportunity to participate in the work of the Harvard Business School stimulated my thinking about a number of problem areas. These areas are reflected in the papers that, revised and integrated, appear in this book, all of which were written during the professorship. Each of these papers is a response to an immediate problem with which I was grappling, either in teaching or consultation, or as a consequence of extended discussion with colleagues. Their continuity lies in the fact that they represent dimensions of my own continuing thinking, based on the same psychological frame of reference, and in the fact that they arise from continuing daily experience. The individually published papers were well received among wide circles of executives, industrial physicians, and colleagues in psychology, psychiatry, and organizational behavior, which of course is pleasing to me. But I am particularly pleased that my Harvard colleagues think them worthy of publication in this book form.

To form an integrated whole, Chapter 1 presents the general frame of reference and my fundamental thesis about motivation.

Chapters 2 and 3 elaborate human needs: the second delineates
the position of my own thinking in the context of contemporary
motivation theory, and the third elaborates that conception to
help the executive reader to increase his awareness of the feelings
I am discussing and their importance. Chapter 4 refers to crises of
becoming and being middle aged. Chapter 5 deals with the costly
experiences of loss. Chapters 6, 7, and 8 are addressed to specific
contemporary problems in which feelings and conflicts of feelings
are paramount. Chapter 9 describes a method of organizational
change to free feelings from artificial constraints and channel
them into problem solving. Chapter 10 delineates some considerations in making use of consultants in organizational change, and
Chapters 11 and 12 contain my summary reflections about the applications of these concepts to the relationship of the executive to
a business school.

I want to express my deep appreciation to former Dean George
P. Baker; Dean Lawrence E. Fouraker, who was previously Director of Research and supported my work in both roles; Senior
Associate Dean George F. F. Lombard; Richard E. Walton, Director of Research, who provided continuing support; and Paul R.
Lawrence and Louis B. Barnes, who, as respective chairmen of
the Organizational Behavior area, were instrumental in my being
invited to come to Harvard, and who provided me with a home
base during my tenure. I also want to thank Margaret Amistadi,
who typed the manuscript, Ellen Friedman, who edited it, and
those students and Faculty members who expanded my horizons,
enriched my professional repertoire, and opened avenues of enduring friendship.

Acknowledgments

I wish to express my thanks as follows to:

The *Harvard Business Review* for permission to adapt the
following articles, which first appeared in that publication:

"On Being a Middle-Aged Manager," July–August 1969,
pp. 51–60.

"A Psychologist Diagnoses Merger Failures," March–April 1970, pp. 139–147.

"Management by Whose Objectives," July–August 1970, pp. 125–134.

"Conflicts That Plague Family Businesses," March–April 1971, pp. 90–98.

"Easing the Pain of Personal Loss," September–October 1972, pp. 80–88.

Copyright 1969, 1970, 1972, by the President and Fellows of Harvard College.

The American Medical Association for permission to adapt the following from the *Archives of Environmental Health*:

"Emotional Toxicity of the Work Environment," August 1969, pp. 239–243.

"Various Approaches to Understanding Man at Work," May 1971, pp. 612–618.

Copyright 1969, 1971 by The American Medical Association.

The American Management Association for permission to adapt "The Quiet Revolution at Foggy Bottom," co-authored by Chris Petrow, Thomas Stern, and me, in *Management Review*, December 1971, pp. 4–14.

Copyright 1971 by The American Management Association.

The American Psychological Association for permission to adapt "The Clinical Psychologist as Organizational Diagnostician," from *Professional Psychology*, Winter 1972, pp. 34–40.

Copyright 1972 by The American Psychological Association.

HARRY LEVINSON

Soldiers Field
Boston, Massachusetts
July 1, 1972

Table of Contents

The Great Jackass Fallacy

CHAPTER 1

The Great Jackass Fallacy

The top management of a large company discovered that some of its line employees had embezzled a five-figure sum while their supervisors had stood by unperturbed. The executives were astonished. They had thought that their supervisors were loyal and that they themselves were thoughtful and kindly. They didn't understand how such thievery could take place in their company.

An airline purchased a fleet of hydraulic lift trucks to put food aboard aircraft. Although they cost hundreds of thousands of dollars, the trucks sat unused on the airport apron. Maintenance employees occasionally glanced at them contemptuously as they went about their work in sullen anger. The company was dismayed that the maintenance men seemed unresponsive to the airline's cost reduction efforts.

Large companies, seeking new products, frequently have bought smaller companies. Almost invariably the successful management of the acquired firm soon departs, and no new products are forthcoming. The larger organization has only increased its size and its managerial burdens. The hoped-for advantages from the merger have evaporated. No one quite knows why this happens repeatedly or why managements don't learn from failures.

When looked at psychologically, the reasons for such occurrences are self-evident. In the first case, every two years the company renegotiated its labor contract. Obviously, the appropriate person to handle the negotiations was the vice president in charge of labor relations. However, the people who actually carried out the contract were first-level supervisors. And they were never asked about what they felt ought to be in the contract or what problems they had in implementing it. By its actions, management effectively communicated to them that they didn't matter much. Furthermore, every two years when the contract came up for renewal, the union let grievances pile up, knowing full well that management would settle them all in the union's favor to get a contract. But the grievances arose when supervisors carried out the terms of the contract. When management gave in, the supervisors felt that they had been undercut. In effect, these people were being told that they were stupid, that they had nothing useful to contribute to policy making, that their job was to do as they were told and that they were expendable when necessary.

In the airline instance, the issue was much the same. A purchasing officer had bought the hydraulic lift trucks, complete with sophisticated electronic controls. What was more natural than for a purchasing officer to do the buying and get the best? But he failed to confer with the mechanics and technicians who would have to keep the trucks operating. After all, what did they know about buying and who asked technicians anyway? Had he asked them, he would have learned that the sophisticated electronic controls were fine for Los Angeles and Phoenix, where the weather was dry and mild, but that they failed repeatedly in New York where the trucks were always exposed to variable, sometimes harsh weather. No matter how hard they worked, the technicians could not keep the trucks functioning. As the supervisors in the previous example, they felt they were being treated contemptuously and were being exploited. Ultimately they gave up trying to keep the trucks going. Seeing how much money the company had wasted on the trucks, they had little incentive to economize in their own small ways.

There are many reasons for merger failures. However, what happens most frequently is that the parent (note the use of that word) company promises its newly acquired company that there will be no sweeping changes. Immediately there are, and the first of these is likely to be in accounting control systems. The flexibility that characterized the smaller, more innovative company is then lost to the control system. Obviously controls are necessary, and just as obviously many small companies do not have *sophisticated* controls. But small companies are frequently flexibly innovative for just that reason. When controls become the central thrust of management, creative people who need flexibility leave, and the parent company is left with a corporate shell. The message received by the acquired company is that the parent company considers it stupid and unsophisticated and therefore the parent must control it more rigidly.

The three situations I have been discussing would be dismissed in most organizations as simply "failures in communications." Many psychologists would advocate dealing with such problems by participative management. However, beneath that glib "explanation," and unresponsive to that ready "remedy," lies a fundamental unconscious attitude that is responsible for most of the contemporary management-labor difficulty and what today is being called a *crisis in motivation*.

CRISIS IN MOTIVATION

The crisis takes many forms: The chief executive of a major company complains about increasing absenteeism, greater inefficiency, and lower productivity. He pointedly reminds his company's employees that their product can be manufactured in Germany and Japan. A news magazine devotes a major story to the inefficiency of American industry, once considered to be the world's most efficient production system. There are mounting vigorous complaints and lawsuits from a whole new movement of now organized and vocal consumers about shoddy products, inadequate services, and marketing deceptions. Companies are repeatedly reorganized on the advice of management consultants to little avail in the long run. New managerial devices, such as the four-day week and putting hourly people on salary, are loudly touted for their effect on employee motivation and morale, but the old problems soon reappear. Efforts to enrich jobs by giving employees more responsibility show encouraging results until employees begin to want to have some voice in company policy and are turned down by management. Students in business schools express a decided preference for smaller businesses. Business and nonprofit organizations alike are burdened by job encumbrances, the product of union-management compromises. Increasing numbers of middle management and professionals, such as engineers, teachers, and hospital personnel, turn toward unionization. Many in the managerial ranks seek new careers, even at lower incomes, that offer the promise of greater individual freedom and initiative.

Most executives with whom I come in contact cannot understand why people don't respond to their executives' efforts to sustain effective organizations, why people seemingly don't want to work, and why people want to leave apparently good organizations. Faced with these problems, often the executives are confused, angry, and hostile to their own people. The terms of chief executives, particularly those in educational and governmental administration, become shorter as the managerial frustrations increase. For example, a recent study by Frederick Harmon of 400 top executives in Europe indicates that they feel menaced.[1] Most see themselves as driving forward toward efficiency but find themselves unsettled by transitions in management styles. They report that they can no longer use the authority of position against subordinates, that they must gain their position by competition with their subordinates and defend that position each step of the way. Sixty-one percent of those interviewed spontaneously mentioned that their main problem was personnel management. Almost all had leadership problems.

The crisis in motivation has long been evident to students of organization who have offered a wide range of theories to cope with it. These are discussed in Chapter 2. Suffice it to say here that by this time, thousands of executives are familiar with these theories. Many have taken part in managerial grids, group dynamics laboratories, seminars on the psychology of management, and a wide range of other forms of training. Some have run the gamut of all training experiences; others have taken up a wide range of less well accepted efforts such as various forms of encounter groups. And some have been enamored of a variety of panaceas offered by quacks.

FAILURE OF RESPONSES

The results of executives' efforts to cope with the crisis in motivation so far have not been impressive. Some companies have tried to

---

[1] Frederick Harmon, "European Top Managers Struggle for Survival," *European Business* (Winter 1971), pp. 14–19.

put the theories into practice with varying success. Some have given up their efforts as too simple for the complexity of the organizational phenomena. Many who have tried to apply the concepts have failed in their efforts or have found no significant differences in their organizational and operational activities. Some have complained that participation in decision making is no remedy, and none of the practices based on these theories offers a cure.

The new theories have confronted executives with the need to distribute power more widely in their organizations, which in turn raises questions about management's right to manage, its responsibility, and its authority. Despite the proliferation of courses and training, as the Harmon study shows, executives now flounder more than ever with respect to the motivational aspects of management. Meanwhile, their power becomes eroded as older methods of control and motivation become less effective.

Why are there such significant gaps between the problems on the one hand and the applications of the theory on the other? The answer to that question is critical for a society comprised of organizations and for a society that depends for its survival on the effective functioning of those organizations. There are, of course, many reasons. First, executives often feel inadequate to apply the concepts. And in that feeling they are frequently right. Managers who have had little or no previous exposure to the behavioral sciences, let alone formal training, can get only the barest introductory knowledge in any brief training program. No one would expect a person to be able to design a complex building after a week-long training program in architecture, nor would he expect it of himself. However, often both the executive and the people who train him expect him to be a different person after he undertakes a week-long sensitivity training laboratory.

Furthermore, it is one thing to learn to become more aware of one's feelings; it is another to do something different about managing them, let alone managing those forces that affect the feelings of other people. If everyone who had experienced psychotherapy were by that fact an expert therapist, there would be no shortage of such healers. Experience is not enough; education in a conceptual framework and supervised skill practice is also required. Many who have expected more of themselves and of brief training experiences are therefore disillusioned, despite the benefits that have often resulted from them.

Would longer training help? Not much, as it is currently conducted, because only a few behavioral scientists are skilled at changing organizations and, therefore, few are in a position to teach executives how to change them. While many behavioral scientists know about the theories, and some practice what is called organizational development, they do not themselves change organizations. Rather, they more often help others think through alternative action possibilities. Many bring groups of employees and executives together and help them overcome the communications barriers toward working out their own solutions. However, unlike marketing experts (who develop and execute marketing programs), and control experts (who install financial control systems), behavioral science experts (with the exception of certain kinds of psychotherapists) are not themselves expert in *doing*. So, more prolonged training is questionable if it does not help executives to develop modes of action.

The second reason for the gap between the problems and the application of solutions is that executives have had insufficient experience in a wide variety of situations to know how to apply conceptions in different ways to different groups and situations. To illustrate, the physician sees the same kinds of illnesses in a variety of patients. He may treat the same illness differently in different patients, depending on their age, physical condition, severity of symptoms, and so on. While executives may work in different organizations, even in different countries, they have insufficient training in the behavioral sciences to attempt to apply more than one or two techniques in all situations. No matter how good those techniques may be, they cannot fit all situations equally well. Furthermore, the behavioral sciences have not yet developed differentiated treatments of choice for changing organizations in the same way physicians have treatments of choice for different illnesses and for the same illness in different patients.

A third problem is that many executives are fearful of losing their control over their organizations. Even though executives encourage their employees to participate in making organizational decisions and in solving organizational problems, and invite people to express themselves more freely, they often feel threatened of their position.

Particularly vulnerable are those executives whose whole life thrust has been to obtain positions of power and control.

Coupled with the fear of losing control is the fact that a disproportionate number of executives are characteristically insensitive to feelings. Many executives have engineering, scientific, legal, and financial or accounting backgrounds. Each of these fields places a heavy emphasis on cognitive rationality and measurable or verifiable facts. People who enter them are usually trained from childhood to suppress their feelings and to maintain a competitive, aggressive, nonemotional front. They are taught to be highly logical, and they seek to impose that kind of rationality on the organizations they encounter. As a result, they simply do not understand the power of human feelings, and all too often such executives are incapable of sensing their own and others' feelings in everyday practice. They are like tone-deaf people who, attending an opera, can understand the lyrics but can't hear the music. Such executives are typified by a company president who was a participant in a seminar on psychological aspects of management. Halfway through the first lecture he broke in to say, "You have already told me more about this subject than I want to know." He was right. Though he stayed to the end of the program, he simply could not grasp what was being taught.

Furthermore, many people pursue executive careers to obtain power over others as a way of compensating for real or fancied personal inadequacies or as a reaction to an unconscious sense of helplessness. Being neurotically driven, their single-minded, perpetual pursuit of control blinds them to their own subtle feelings and to those of others.

Still another reason for the gap between the problems and their resolution lies in union attitudes. Union leaders, too, are afraid of any practice that might undermine their power. Most have long since given up any ideology that emphasizes values other than wages, hours, and working conditions. Even when unions are not opposed to innovative means of coping with motivational issues, managers fear that they are and back away.

All of these reasons, coupled with the inadequacies of contemporary theory, explain much of the disparity between theory and practice. In time, with new knowledge and better training experiences, most of these weaknesses will be overcome. But the fact remains that much more effort could be applied now than is being applied even with present knowledge. Obviously there is another, more subtle barrier, one that will inhibit the application of whatever further knowledge is developed. This barrier is an unconscious assumption about motivation, held particularly by executives in all types of organizations and reinforced by organizational theories and structures. I call it the great jackass fallacy.

THE GREAT JACKASS FANTASY

Frequently, when conducting executive seminars, I ask the participants what the dominant philosophy of motivation in American management is. Almost invariably, they quickly agree that it is the carrot-and-stick philosophy: reward and punishment. Then I ask them to close their eyes for a moment and to form a picture in their mind's eye with a carrot at one end and a stick at the other. When they have done so I ask them to describe the central image in that picture. Most frequently they respond that the central figure is a jackass.

When the first image that comes to mind when one thinks "carrot-and-stick" is a jackass, obviously the unconscious assumption behind the reward-punishment model is that one is dealing with jackasses, that people are jackasses to be manipulated and controlled. Thus, unconsciously, the boss is the manipulator and controller, and the subordinate is the jackass.

The characteristics of a jackass are stubbornness, stupidity, willfulness, and unwillingness to go where someone is driving him. These, by interesting coincidence, are also the characteristics of the unmotivated employee. Thus it becomes vividly clear that the underlying assumption management unconsciously makes about motivation leads to a self-fulfilling prophecy. People will inevitably respond to the carrot-and-stick by trying to get more of the carrot and by protecting themselves against the stick. This predictable phenomenon led to the formation of unions and to the frequent sabotage of management's incentive efforts as well as to the characteristic employees' suspicion of management's motivational (manipulative) techniques. Employees obviously sense the carrot-and-stick conception behind management's attitudes and just as obviously respond to the communications built around those attitudes with appropriate self-defending measures.

There is much talk about the need to improve communications in all organizations. However, the problem all too often is not that communication is inadequate but, rather, that it is too explicit. When people sense themselves to be viewed as jackasses, they will automatically resist hearing management's messages, no matter how clear the type or how pretty the pictures. Most managerial communications to employees, therefore, are a waste of time and money.

Since the turn of the century, half a dozen different philosophies of management have appeared, each emphasizing a different dimension of the management task, and each advocating a new set of techniques. Though they differ from each other in many respects, all are based on reward-punishment psychology. Almost all of the contemporary psychological conceptions of motivation (discussed in Chapter 2) take a reward-punishment psychology for granted, and they fail to see the contradiction between advocating trust and openness among employees and managers on the one hand and, on the other, accepting the thesis that the more powerful people have a natural right to manipulate the less powerful.

But as long as anyone in a leadership role operates with reward-punishment assumptions about motivation, he is implicitly assuming that he has (or should have) control over others and that they are in a jackass position with respect to him. Such a relationship is inevitably one of condescending contempt whose most blatant mask is paternalism. The result of that psychological position is a continuing battle between those who seek to wield power and those who are subject to it, as reflected in the Harmon study referred to earlier, and in the history of labor-management relations. The consequences are increased inefficiency, lowered productivity, heightened absenteeism, and other modes of withdrawal from engagement in that kind of relationship, or covert engagement in a combative struggle.

BUREAUCRATIC COMPLICATIONS

The problems resulting from the underlying jackass fallacy are compounded further by bureaucratic organizational structure. A bureaucratic structure is based on a military model that assumes control of the organization from the bottom up by whoever is at the top. In pure form it is a rigid hierarchy, complete with detailed job descriptions and fixed measurable objectives. Such a structure requires everyone at every level to be dependent on those at higher levels. Hiring, firing, promotion, demotion, reassignment, and similar actions are the prerogatives of superiors who can make such decisions unilaterally. In short, a subordinate's fate is decided by a distant "they" whom he frequently does not know (individuals who are beyond his influence, let alone his control). Such circumstances make for increasing defensiveness on the part of the subordinate, for he must protect himself against being manipulated and against the feeling of helplessness that inevitably accompanies dependency. Rank and file employees have long since counteracted this defenselessness by unionizing. Managerial and professional employees are beginning to follow suit, and that trend will continue to grow.

While the bureaucratic structure with its heavy emphasis on internal competition for power and position is often touted as a device for achievement, it is actually a system built for defeat. Fewer people move up the pyramidal hierarchy at each step. That leaves a residual of failures, often euphemistically called "career people," who thereafter are passed over because they have not succeeded in the competition for managerial positions. Most such people feel resentful and defeated. Often they have been manipulated or judged arbitrarily. They constitute a heavy burden in most organizations for they are no longer motivated by competitive spirit: the carrots-and-sticks mean less. There is little need in their eyes to learn more; they simply do as they are told. They usually stay until retirement and are frequently described as the "deadwood" that needs to be cleaned out when a new management takes over.

Executives new to a company or to higher level jobs like to think of themselves as being effective in cleaning out the deadwood or trimming the excess managerial fat. Some take to that task with great vigor. Unfortunately the consequences are more negative than enthusiastic executives like to recognize. In one large company where just that task was undertaken with the hope that the 40-year-olds would respond with unbridled enthusiasm when the 50-year-olds were cleaned out, the younger men failed to respond. They saw in what was happening to the older men their likely fate in ten years.

Bureaucratic structure, with its implicit power struggle orientation, increases infighting, empire building, rivalry, and the sense of futility. It tends to magnify latent feelings that the organization is a hostile environment that people can do little to change. Little wonder that many young people do not want to get caught up in such struggles. Since 90 percent of workers work in organizations, most young people, too, must do so. But they would rather be in organizations that provide them with an opportunity to demonstrate their competence and proficiency than in those that test their ability to run a managerial maze successfully.

These two factors—the great jackass fallacy and the bureaucratic organization structure—are formidable obstacles to organizational survival. They are essentially self-defeating, if what an executive wants from his followers in an organization is spontaneity, investment, dedication, commitment, affiliation, and adaptive innovation. As already indicated, many executives try to cope with the pathology of the system by introducing new techniques, such as group dynamics or job enrichment. These are simply palliatives in an organization that has few effective ways of integrating them; when people are asked to express their feelings more freely and to take on greater responsibility, they soon come into conflict with power centers and power figures in a system geared to the acquisition of power. The latter soon cry, "Business is not a democracy." Such efforts then are quickly shed and disillusionment sets in once again, both on the part of the management that tried the new techniques and the subordinates who were involved in them.

Unless the fundamental assumptions of management (and behavioral scientists) about motivation are changed and unless the organizational structure is changed to match the changing assumptions about motivation, then the underlying jackass assumptions will remain visible to those who are subjected to them no matter what practices the organization undertakes. People will avoid, evade, escape, deny, and reject both the jackass assumption and the military style hierarchy, for few people can tolerate being a jackass in a psychological prison without doing something about it.

This issue is critically important for society as a whole because society is increasingly made up of organizations. The less effectively organizations carry out the work of society, the greater the cost in money and in social paralysis. This paralysis leads to the kind of de-moralization already evident in problems of transportation, health care, education and welfare, and motivation.

BEGINNING ALTERNATIVE STEPS

If the executive leader grasps the import of what I am saying, shudders appropriately, and wants to do something else, what are his alternatives? Is he forever doomed to play with psychological gim-micks? Is he himself so much a victim of his assumptions that he can-not change them? I don't think this is necessarily so for the majority of executives. I think there are viable alternatives. I would offer the following suggestions as points of departure:

(1) Anyone who supervises anyone else should look carefully at the as-sumptions he is making about motivation. He must assess for him-self how strongly carrot-and-stick assumptions are implicit in his own attitudes. One may argue that if he tries to be nice to people the stick is softened. No matter. He is still operating with carrot-and-stick. Paternalistic kindness is only a disguised form of carrot-and-stick which seeks to increase loyalty by creating guilt in those who are the recipients of managerial largesse.

(2) Having honestly and frankly faced up to one's own assumption about what makes people tick, the next step is to look at one's or-ganizational structure. Most organizations are constructed to fit a hierarchical model. People assume that the hierarchical organiza-tional structure is to organizations as the spine is to human beings, that it is both necessary and given. As a matter of fact, it is not al-ways necessary nor is it a given. This is not to argue that there shouldn't be distribution of power and control, but, rather, that it need not take this particular form. Every executive should ask him-self, "Is my organization organized for hierarchical structure or is my structure organized to accomplish the task the organization must do?" If it is organized more to fit the hierarchical model than for the task, it is time to consider what other organization model might be better able to accomplish the desired tasks.[2]

(3) Implicit in whatever organizational structure one evolves is an as-sumption about what makes people tick. Therefore it is important to look very carefully at what are the most powerful motivations. In

---

[2] Paul R. Lawrence and Jay W. Lorsch, *Organization and Environment* (Boston: Harvard University Graduate School of Business Administration, Division of Research, 1967).

Chapter 2, I shall trace the development of theoretical conceptions about motivation as they relate to management and delineate my own position in contrast to the currently accepted psychological conventions. In Chapter 3, I shall make a simple extrapolation of these conceptions to illuminate and illustrate the ways in which the work environment becomes emotionally toxic to people and what managers and companies might do about minimizing that toxicity. In Chapters 4 and 5 I shall apply the same model to the normal crises of normal individuals—the fact of middle age and the daily losses of support, affection, and self-esteem that we all experience. Then in Chapters 6, 7, and 8 I shall turn to three topics that have appeared with increasing frequency during my Harvard years: the problems of objectives, merger, and family businesses. While these certainly do not cover the range of organizational problems nor are they meant to be a systematic treatment of all organizational problems, nevertheless, by reviewing these three very common issues that are among the most complex and difficult which managers have to face, the fundamental elements of my theory and its possible helpfulness in dealing with these issues can then be seen more clearly against the context of operational reality. Organizational change is a perennial and pressing issue. In Chapter 9, I shall use one case and one method to illustrate the applicability and usefulness of the theory and other facets of its conception in dealing with the most difficult kind of organizational change.

Having illustrated the theoretical conceptions and their application in these various modes, I shall, in Chapter 10, issue some cautions and raise some questions about the glib application of organizational change efforts. In Chapter 11, I shall apply the conceptions in the form of a reflection about business school students.

While the chapters, having originally been discrete papers, jump from topic to topic, they nevertheless serve to illuminate the range of my frame of reference, hopefully to demonstrate both its consistency and its validity while simultaneously offering constructive and creative modes for dealing with some of the more severe contemporary problems of management.

CONCLUSION

In sum, I contend that the increasing momentum toward demotivation in contemporary American culture is a product of the carrot-and-stick philosophy and the hierarchical organization structure, both of which imprison people psychologically and assume that they are jackasses to be manipulated. This self-fulfilling prophecy has destructive effects on the competitive enterprise system in a free society because the alienation it produces from common purposes and common goals is at the core of our social and organizational rot. I contend that effective management must get rid of this invalid motivational assumption and revise the anachronistic organizational structure in order to recapture the momentum toward unlimited possibilities and stimulate the inherent potential of people and their willingness to solve problems, to achieve goals, and to reach for the stars. This I see as the fundamental challenge of the leadership of all types of institutions and organizations.

CHAPTER 2

Various Approaches to
Understanding Man at Work

THE MANAGERIAL WOODS ARE FULL of theories and fads. A psychologist, whose basic training is in the understanding of the individual and in methods to help him restore his adaptive equilibrium, necessarily comes to the study of organizations and the motivation of people in organizations with that same frame of reference. That is, he will look upon theories and fads for the degree to which they reflect an understanding of the psychology of the individual and the equilibrium maintaining efforts of both individuals and organizations. Individuals do not lose their individuality because they are in groups or organizations, and the latter are necessarily made up of individuals. Just as one cannot deny physiochemical processes because he is studying biology, so one cannot deny individual psychological processes because he is studying motivation in and related to management.

The task of adapting myself to a new field, namely the psychology of management, has required that I take a critical, analytic look at theories and fads, to understand how they came about and with what assumptions they operated, so that I could then formulate and state for myself my own position. And it was that effort that led to the formulation expressed in this chapter, culminating in the conception of *psychological man,* on which I elaborate after reviewing historic and contemporary trends and concepts. This conception of psychological man—whose crucial sources of motivation are imbedded in his efforts to adapt to his world—is fundamental for me and sets the frame of reference for all of the subsequent chapters. Since all executives struggle with motivational issues and may have also struggled with the same problem of conflicting theories and fads, perhaps they will find this discussion stimulating for their own thinking, whether or not they agree with mine.

Any effort to understand man at work and obtain a perspective on contemporary theory and practice related to work motivation must begin with the roots of both subjects. All discussions of the meaning of work and the motivation to work are the product of four interacting forces: (1) a theory of psychological motivation; (2) the major social role encompassed in the concept of work at any given time; (3) a conception of the modal organization structure within which people work; and (4) a view of the broader ethos within which work organization functions.

Contemporary theory and practice may then be viewed as an outcome of these four forces. With such a perspective, the shortcomings of theory and practice may be clarified. These shortcomings may then be appreciated as the inevitable concomitant of evolutionary steps that are perpetually entangled in outmoded notions and struggling to accommodate to new ones.

THEORIES OF MOTIVATION

Two major conceptions of man dominated psychological thinking in the nineteenth and twentieth centuries. One conception, with a tradition stemming from Locke through Watson to Skinner, is an *outside,* or environmental, theory of motivation. It views man's motivation and behavior as shaped primarily by forces outside himself. It is largely an empirical theory that leads to research focused on forces and factors external to the person, and is correspondingly less concerned with such internal factors as thinking, feelings, and subjective experiences.

The second conception is a nativistic, or *inside,* theory of motivation. In its more modern form it stems from Kant, and its two most widely known contemporary names are Freud and Piaget. Nativistic conceptions see man as unfolding and developing physiologically and psychologically from biologically based givens. They focus on the development and refinement of internal capacities, primarily emotional and cognitive, which give rise to certain feelings, wishes, fantasies, perceptions, attitudes, and thoughts.

Research and practice based on environmental theories tend to be concerned with the *control* of behavior, implicitly assuming someone is controlled and someone else is controlling. Referring to work motivation, the question usually is asked, "How can the employee *be* motivated?" Often the implication is that by doing something to the person or his environment, he can be made to do, by someone else, what is either desired or expected of him.

Research and practice based on nativistic theories tend to be concerned with *understanding* behavior and often with freeing a person to behave more nearly in keeping with his wishes or with opening a wider range of choices from which he presumably may choose alternative courses. Managerial practice based on nativistic theory related to work motivation seeks to understand the person's own motivations and to create conditions under which these can flower in the work situation to meet the needs of both the person and the organization.

MAJOR WORK ROLE

Until the industrial revolution, the major work role was that of laborer or artisan. To work was largely to do something with one's hands with varying degrees of skill. Comparatively few did commercial, intellectual, professional, political, or military work. Even the prophets of the Old Testament were artisans. The laborer-artisan usually worked alone or in a small group.

The industrial revolution made a machine-tender of the worker. Often the machine had greater skill and competence than the man. Large numbers of men had to be brought together to operate numbers of machines in plants. The paradigmatic working man was a factory employee who became heavily dependent upon the employing organization, often for a working lifetime. The growth of a factory culture led to the expansion of cities and the proliferation of material goods. The development of cities destroyed the supportive resources of the extended family and small town, requiring development of service roles to replace those losses.

Ultimately the plethora of material goods from the factory culture lessened pressure for continuous work, providing higher incomes and greater leisure, which called for more service functions as standards of living and expectations of service were raised. In the West we are presently midway between a factory and a service culture; many predict that soon men will not have to tend machines. Service will become the modal work role. Services may be offered by individuals or organizations but, because of their complexity, will tend largely to be rendered by organizations. Medical service is an example.

Beyond service as the modal work role lies involvement. Involvement as a modal work role means that people are engaged together in joint problem-solving for their mutual benefit and for the good of society. Involvement requires a multiplicity of specialized skills which can be brought together but need not be held together once the problems for which they were assembled are solved. We are just at the beginning of the involvement stage. For all practical purposes, involvement will have to take place within social institutions, for contemporary social problem solving is done by institutions and organizations rather than by individuals. Today's problems are outcomes of system functioning and must be solved by working with such systems. For example, today conservation means one must cope with pollution, housing, transportation, and many other factors.

ORGANIZATION STRUCTURE

The earliest organizational structures within which work was accomplished were families, extended kinship systems, tribes, or villages. Work in such structures was inseparable from other aspects of living, for living was largely a process of sustaining an all-too-short life. Early elements of bureaucratic structure were found in the Western world in the only nonfamily work, the church and the military.

The industrial revolution, with its more finely differentiated work roles and responsibilities and work areas located away from the home, gave rise to formal bureaucratic structures in which tasks were defined, responsibilities assigned, and authority delegated. The underlying assumption of a bureaucratic structure is that the head of the organization has control and the followers respond to the command and direction of the leader or his delegates.

Bureaucratic structures lend themselves well to factory culture and the derivatives of feudal conceptions of authority, obligation, and loyalty, which define the complementary relationships of the more and less powerful. However, bureaucratic structures are essentially static. They work well to the extent that people can be contained and controlled within them and work can be routinized. The less people can be contained within a physical place, the less control can be exerted over them; the less routine the work, the less well bureaucratic structures function.

When service is the modal form of work, requiring as it does varied but complementary skills, supervision and control by authority are less possible because a greater complexity of function means authority figures can no longer possess all skills or exercise all competencies. Those in authority must depend on the skilled individuals doing the work to exercise the necessary competence as responsible individual partners. This is the point Galbraith makes in discussing the infrastructures of organizations which, for all practical purposes, make organizational decisions.[1] Furthermore, the more flexible an organization must be to adapt to its environment, the more freedom people must have to make decisions at the point of action, which, in large measure, mitigates the central control possibilities of bureaucratic structures. In addition, bureaucratic structures operate on a unit-efficiency basis. They compute their efficiency by counting units produced during a given period of time. This measure is less useful when the assembly line is not the prototype of work, when the work to be done is of a project nature and is a task to be accomplished rather than a number of pieces to be made.

Organizations that are structured to render service or solve problems require more coordination and mutual interaction. Those people who actually render the service wield great power at the point of service. They are not as interchangeable as machine tenders. Standards of performance are as much those of the profession or discipline as of the organizations through which the services are rendered. Loyalty tends to be divided between the professional reference group and the organization, as in medicine, nursing, and engineering. The standard of performance is the excellence of task accomplishment. Service and problem-solving organizations tend more to be made up

---

[1] John Kenneth Galbraith, *The New Industrial State* (Boston: Houghton Mifflin, 1967).

of units that can be readily organized, disorganized, and reorganized in keeping with tasks to be done. Project organizations or matrix organizations (in which there are overlapping functions) are more common modes of rendering services and solving problems. Since these cannot be held together by bureaucratic controls, they must depend for cohesiveness on common purpose and on the identification of the employees with the organizational goals. The less the bureaucratic control, the more the organization must depend on voluntary commitment for accomplishing organizational tasks. Thus, control is inevitably much more self-control, control by peers and the requirements of the task. When bureaucratic controls are lessened, authority figures are more influenced by and responsive to others in the structure.

Organization structures may take a variety of forms. Ultimately we will see many different organizational structures in the same company as structure more closely follows function.

ETHOS

The combination of assumptions about motivation, about the modal social role of work, and about the structure of organizations, with the dominant economic theories of an era, comprise the ethos within which managerial theory and practice evolve. Beginning with the industrial revolution, overlapping phases may be distinguished, each characterized by a dominant ethos.

Economic Man

The first major phase was that of economic man. The underlying assumption about motivation was environmental, specifically that man was rational and economic in his outlook and that he would be motivated by money. Man, like the machines he operated or the tasks he did in a bureaucratic structure, was viewed as an interchangeable part. Further, he existed to serve the organization. His feelings, if considered at all, were viewed as annoyances in an otherwise rational, organized, controlled system. The dominant mode of motivation was by appeal to presumably obvious reason, backed up by the carrot-and-stick. The greater wisdom of superiors in the hierarchy was taken for granted, and a worker's economic fate was dependent on their greater knowledge and power.

Most contemporary managements still operate primarily in the economic man ethos. While organizations may be more or less paternalistic in an effort to obtain loyalty and commitment, most seek greater efficiency by breaking jobs down into the smallest possible work units and expect to motivate employees by financial reward. Most industrial sociology and organizational theory are concerned with describing bureaucratic structure, assuming it as a given and also assuming a reward-punishment model of individual motivation. Most industrial psychology, with its emphasis on testing, selection, placement, reward, supervision, morale and motivation, is heavily environmental in its underlying motivational assumptions.

Social Man

The second major phase was that of social man. It arose largely from the work of Elton Mayo and his colleagues.[2] Mayo called attention to the importance of social relationships in organizations, giving rise to considerable work on informal social organization and group norms and calling into question the economic man model. While Mayo focused on man's need for affiliation with his fellows, and thus began to take a nativistic direction, he did not question seriously the bureaucratic model or look closely at other aspects of internal motivation. Mayo saw interpersonal relationships as primary and work as secondary. His work stimulated attention to supervisor-supervisee relationships and work group interactions and gave impetus to the human relations movement in industry. It led also to criticism of the ennui of factory work and to efforts at job enlargement to make the work place more congenial and, sometimes, to paternalism.

Mayo's conception flatly contradicted the economic man model. Those who followed him did not contradict him. Their thinking may be seen as elaborations of the social man conception.

---

[2] Elton Mayo, *The Human Problems of an Industrial Civilization* (New York: Macmillan, 1933); F. J. Roethlisberger and W. J. Dickson, *Management and the Worker* (Cambridge, Mass.: Harvard University Press, 1939); W. J. Dickson and F. J. Roethlisberger, *Counseling in an Organization* (Boston: Harvard University Graduate School of Business Administration, Division of Research, 1966).

Self-Actualizing Man

The third major phase, building on Mayo, but more a product of the followers of Kurt Lewin,[3] is that of self-actualizing man. With philosophical roots in Rousseau and Ruskin, the proponents of self-actualizing man saw him as spontaneous, creative, and seeking self-expression. They sought to free the working man from the constraints of bureaucracy and unilateral power. They continued to view work as a necessity but contended that it need not be psychologically destructive to the worker. Furthermore, they pointed out that what seemed efficient in the bureaucratic model of economic man was really less efficient, because control by hierarchical relationships and industrial engineering not only dehumanized man but required him to defend himself against such controls by passive resistance and reluctance to be involved in the system. In fact, between the lines of conceptions of self-actualizing man is the notion that organizations exist to serve man rather than vice versa. There followed the converse emphasis on actualization of potential and reduction of power differentials in bureaucratic structures.

For example, the late Douglas McGregor [4] suggested that managements operated by what he called Theory X: the assumption that (1) the average human being has an inherent dislike of work and will avoid it if he can; (2) therefore most people must be coerced, controlled, directed, and threatened to put forth adequate effort; (3) the average human being prefers to be directed, wishes to avoid responsibility, has relatively little ambition, wants security above all.

Opposed to these assumptions he offered what he called Theory Y: (1) the expenditure of physical and mental effort in work is as natural as play or rest; (2) man will exercise self-direction and self-control in the service of objectives to which he is committed; (3) commitment to objectives is a function of the rewards associated with their achievement, the most significant rewards being the satisfaction of self-actualizing needs; (4) the average human being learns, under proper conditions, not only to accept but to seek responsibility; (5)

---

[3] Kurt Lewin, *Field Theory in Social Science* (New York: Harper & Row, 1951).

[4] Douglas McGregor, *The Human Side of Enterprise* (New York: McGraw-Hill, 1960).

the capacity to exercise a relatively high degree of imagination, ingenuity, and creativity in the solution of organizational problems is widely distributed in the population; (6) under conditions of modern industrial life, the intellectual potentialities of the average human being are only partially utilized.

McGregor's position is largely nativistic, holding that man's needs are primarily social and egoistic. He holds work to be a natural expenditure of energy and commitment originating from esteem and self-actualization. Commitment frees people to be imaginative, self-disciplined, responsible, and cooperative. McGregor envisions the possibility of integrating individual and organizational goals and emphasizes interpersonal relationships and flexibility of organizational structure.

Chris Argyris, too, seeks to integrate individual and organizational needs.[5] He sees bureaucratic structure as inhibiting the fulfillment of individual needs, particularly those for a sense of personal value, self-esteem, and independence. Like McGregor, he views individuals as self-motivated rather than motivated by forces outside themselves. Both McGregor and Argyris advocate sensitivity training as a medium for obtaining openness, cooperation, and commitment.

Rensis Likert conceives of an organization as comprised of interacting small groups that ideally have great autonomy and are linked together by "linking pins" (that is, key management personnel who are members of two groups), into an integrated whole.[6] He gives heavy emphasis to small group interaction and to that between superiors and subordinates. He advocates group accountability, consensus decision, and group goal setting. His major theme is that the principle of supportive relationships is basic to a sense of personal worth and importance.

Blake and Mouton, too, see no necessary conflict between individual and organizational objectives.[7] They emphasize managerial style as the major device for counteracting bureaucracy. They have popularized what they call the "managerial grid," a two-dimensional tem-

---

[5] Chris Argyris, *Integrating the Individual and the Organization* (New York: John Wiley & Sons, 1964).

[6] Rensis Likert, *New Patterns in Management* (New York: McGraw-Hill, 1961).

[7] Robert R. Blake and Jane S. Mouton, *The Managerial Grid* (Houston: Gulf Publishing Co., 1964).

plate on which executives can scale themselves according to their degree of concern for people and for production. This presumably provides managers with insight into their own behavior, and with a heavy emphasis on interpersonal relationships. Blake and Mouton have supplemented their scale with self-administered exercises and teaching devices, derived from sensitivity training, which illuminate intraorganizational conflicts.

The work of Frederick Herzberg on motivation through work itself, though he is not strictly a Lewinian, emphasizes job enrichment.[8] Herzberg conceives of "satisfiers" and "dissatisfiers." Satisfiers are achievement, recognition, the work itself, responsibility, advancement, and growth. Dissatisfiers include company policy and administration, supervision, working conditions, interpersonal relationships (with superiors, subordinates, and peers), salary, status, job security, and personal life. Satisfiers are motivating; dissatisfiers cannot motivate people to work but can counteract motivation. In Herzberg's conception they are hygienic factors that can contaminate the psychological environment. Herzberg, like Argyris, urges management to increase the challenging aspects of the job to make it more self-fulfilling, achievement-motivated, and self-actualizing. Although Herzberg does not follow the model of economic man, he assumes that *higher management* should enrich the jobs of lower level people. He raises few questions about organizational structure, controls, or power relationships, and he minimizes interpersonal relationships as motivating forces. Work must be given meaning largely by expanding responsibility and extending recognition as well as from the intrinsic satisfaction the person derives from it.

All of the theories discussed lean heavily on the concept of a hierarchy of needs put forth by the late Abraham Maslow.[9] Maslow contended that human needs could be classified on five levels, each succeeding need becoming more pressing as more primitive ones were satisfied. In ascending order these are physiological needs, safety needs, needs for belonging and love, need for esteem, and need for self-actualization.

---

[8] Frederick Herzberg, *Work and the Nature of Man* (Cleveland: World Publishing Co., 1966).

[9] Abraham Maslow, *Motivation and Personality* (New York: Harper & Row, 1954).

The emphasis of this body of theory gave rise to such conceptions as participation in decision making, more adequate support from higher level management, and responsible involvement in the work itself and in decisions about how it was to be done. Questions began to be raised about organizational structure. The group dynamics movement brought into vogue emphasis on open communication, partnership with respect to task accomplishment, and the reduction of psychological barriers to cooperation. The fundamental thrust of this phase complemented the increasing trend toward service work and involvement.

However, most of these efforts are still based on a reward-punishment psychology, where a person's needs are seen normatively as broad categories of generalized need, such as achievement and self-actualization, with little differentiation among different people and different circumstances. While these theorists gave more attention to nativistic man, they were largely without a systematic theory of personality on which to base conceptions of need. Often they implicitly saw man as having limited motivational dimensions and frequently tried to force nativistic conceptions into organizations that were based fundamentally on environmental assumptions. However, as a result of their influence, many companies are now trying to assimilate and act on the model of self-actualizing man.

Psychological Man

The fourth major phase, now in its elementary beginnings, is that of psychological man. This concept is based on a comprehensive theory of personality. Stemming largely from psychoanalytic conceptions, it views man as a complex, unfolding, maturing organism who passes through physiological and psychological stages of development, as an open system interacting with his environment. Man evolves an ego ideal toward which he strives and a complex set of mechanisms and defenses for coping with the basic drives of sexuality and aggression, with the superego or conscience, and with the environment. Work serves different purposes for different people, but for all it is a major device to maintain psychological equilibrium. This view holds that the major spontaneous human effort is that of adaptation, which means aggressive attack on the environment to master it for survival. These notions about personality functioning are far more complex than the general rubric of self-actualization. For example, in this concept of psychological man, self-esteem is related to ego ideal and to the whole of personality theory. The relationship of a man to the organization in which he works becomes of critical psychological importance. The organization psychologically recapitulates the family structure of the culture in which it is found, and employees evolve both conscious and unconscious psychological contracts with organizations as devices to maintain their psychological equilibria. While these considerations militate against the rigidity of historic bureaucracy, they recognize the importance of leadership and power relationships and see danger in vitiating power positions or undermining the leadership role. Although some people still see work as onerous or even as a form of slavery and look forward to the age of leisure, this kind of comprehensive psychological conception sees work as a mode of mastery of self and environment. In this view, though man may be freer from compulsion and physical labor, he will never be free of work.

In contrast to the humanistic, self-actualizing theories of motivation which are derived largely from academic conceptions of personality, the considerably more complex psychological theories of motivation are derived from insights originally based on clinical work with individuals, largely by clinical psychologists and psychiatrists. These theories are heavily nativistic in that they place strong emphasis on the conception that man is continuously balancing his sexual and aggressive drives, the pressures and demands of his superego or conscience, and the realities of his world in his effort to master himself and it. This view is also environmentalistic because the focus is not with man alone or with organization alone but significantly with the man-organization relationship. The major theorists of this point of view are Elliott Jaques, Abraham Zaleznik, and I.

Jaques is concerned with two areas: superior-subordinate relationships, modes through which employees can express their power constructively with respect to policies; and practices of salary administration, which enable employees to compare their level of pay with that of other groups whom they judge to be carrying equivalent levels of responsibility.[10] Jaques seeks to cope with the employee's sense

---

[10] Elliott Jaques, *Work, Creativity and Social Justice* (New York: International Universities Press, 1970).

of insecurity and the stirring of his unconscious anxieties when contemporary threats and problems reawaken repressed childhood conflicts that then lead to irrational behavior.

Zaleznik directs most of his attention to the special psychological problems facing people who become organizational leaders and to the psychological forces that compel people to invent systems of organizing work that then influence society and thereby affect other people.[11] He and his students have investigated the ways in which the unconscious motives of individuals affect decision making. In addition, he has emphasized the capacity of the individual to mold his own life, both at work and at home. That emphasis on what the individual can do to act responsibly to control his own destiny contrasts with the humanists' appeal to enlightened management.

My own conception is built around an ego psychology model. I have defined the three broad classes of needs to be met as (1) ministration needs—for care and support from others—(2) maturation needs—for growth and development—and (3) mastery needs—for control of one's fate—allowing considerable variation in the definition of such needs for different individuals and groups of people.[12]

My fundamental thesis is that the most powerful motivating force for any human being is his wish to attain his ego ideal. In the course of growing up, out of our identifications with our parents, out of our wish to emulate them, out of the encouragement and affection of our teachers and other people who are important to us, out of the refinements of our skills and competencies, we evolve a picture for ourselves of how we should be at our ideal best. When we work toward our ideal best we like ourselves; when we come close we are elated. When we do not, we become extremely angry with ourselves.

One has only to think of how he criticizes himself for the simple accident of spilling a drink at the table to see how harsh we are to ourselves for trivial mistakes—errors that keep us from being as perfect in our own eyes as we would like to be. Adults in North American society (and probably most others) like to see themselves as com-

---

[11] Abraham Zaleznik, *The Human Dilemmas of Leadership* (New York: Harper & Row, 1966).

[12] Harry Levinson, *The Exceptional Executive* (Cambridge, Mass.: Harvard University Press, 1968).

petent and effective in doing well what they do. They are unhappy with themselves when they do poorly or inadequately. The reasons are very simple. One's self-esteem is a product of the gap between his ego ideal and his self-image. The greater the gap, the more he dislikes himself and the angrier and the more self-critical he becomes with himself. Indeed we are then ridden with extremely uncomfortable feelings of inadequacy and guilt.

Why then do people do sloppy work? Why are they absent? Why are they unmotivated? Largely out of anger and out of need to protect themselves. Many such people have low self-images and, therefore, low self-esteem because they are caught up in the carrot-and-stick motivational conception and the military general-staff hierarchical model. To raise their self-esteem, they must fight back and they do so, even at the risk of hurting themselves, by producing shoddy goods, leaving jobs and, in effect, telling the organization to go to hell.

Thus the individual is most highly motivated to meet the demands of his own ego ideal, his wish to attain that perfection that represents himself at his ideal future best. To meet this internal demand, he must manage the twin drives of sex and aggression and the four major feelings or wishes derived from them: feelings of love and of hate and dependency wishes on the one hand, and the wish to master the environment on the other.

Therefore I view a man's relationship to his work and to his work organization as part of his generalized effort to meet the demands of his ego ideal and, as a result, to be significantly related both to his emotional health and his motivation at work. The kind of work he does and the nature of his relationship to the organization either supports his personality structure and enables him to use himself psychologically as he would like to do, thereby enhancing both his motivation and his health, or it impairs both.

Thus I do not see bureaucracy as either good or bad by definition, for some tasks require bureaucratic structure and some people need more structured organizational support than others to satisfy their dependency needs. I take seriously the psychological interaction of the person and his organization and the psychological usefulness of organizational structure.

I am therefore much interested in organizational design, particularly the work of Lawrence and Lorsch,[13] which promises a method for evolving a sophisticated understanding of organizational functioning, comparable in depth to and compatible with psychoanalytical theory. Lawrence and Lorsch point out that it is necessary to differentiate different parts of an organization in terms of their formal characteristics and their climate characteristics. Different kinds of work require different patterns of formal relationships and duties, different patterns of formal rules and procedures and control and measurement systems, and have different time dimensions and different goals. A sales department would differ in these respects from a research department. Such differences could be delineated in terms of the kinds of work styles, values, and skills, and the types of personalities required to carry on such activities successfully. By differentiating the work environments more clearly in behavioral and emotional terms, a better fit can then be made between the individual and the work organization to enable him to achieve a greater sense of mastery and to better meet the demands of his ego ideal.

I am particularly interested in the leadership role, which I consider to be more complex and active than do most of the other theorists. If all organizations in any society are essentially recapitulations of the family structure in that society, then the leader is psychologically in a father figure role (that is, he encounters unconscious expectations that he behave in the modal way a father behaves in his culture) that he must understand and act upon to ensure the perpetuation of the organization.

Conceptions of psychological man, in the sense used here, have yet to be implemented in any significant way. They call for viewing the organization as an adaptive organism directed to its own perpetuation.[14] Thus conceived, an organization is a problem-solving mechanism. It is an educational institution that, for its own survival, must increase the psychological and economic competence of those who work in it. This conception calls for a different role for the leader, that of a teacher of problem solving and a facilitator of human development.

This more complex conception requires deeper, more comprehen-

---

[13] Paul R. Lawrence and Jay W. Lorsch, *Organization and Environment* (Boston: Harvard University Graduate School of Business Administration, Division of Research, 1967).

[14] Levinson, *The Exceptional Executive.*

TABLE 2-1

Schematic Recapitulation of Approaches to Understanding Man at Work

Theory of Motivation	Major Work Role	Organization Structure	Ethos	Advocates
Outside	Laborer, artisan	Families, kinship systems	Economic man	Managers, economists, industrial engineers
	Machine tender	Bureaucratic	Social man	Mayo, human relations school
Inside	Service	Project, matrix	Self-Actualizing man	Neo-Lewinians, humanistic psychologists, organizational sociologists
Inside-Outside	Involvement	Multiform	Psychological man	Psychoanalytically trained psychologists and psychiatrists

sive understanding of motivation as a complex derived from drives, wishes, fantasies, and the ego ideal. That requires a more sophisticated understanding of organizations, one only now slowly evolving.[15] Ultimately it will be possible to fit men to organizations and vice versa by differentiating the psychological components of work performance and organizational structure and matching these with personality configurations.

All of the theories under the rubric of psychological man presume a modal work role of involvement.

CONCLUSION

Managerial theory and practice related to work motivation are necessarily based on assumptions about motivation in general. They presuppose a theory of personality, a modal view of the work role and the work organization, and the ethos of work (see Table 2-1). In my judgment, most contemporary theory and practice fall short of their possibilities because they are not adequately based on a comprehensive theory of personality, and they fail to take into account the need for differentiating organizational structure to meet the needs defined by such a comprehensive theory of personality.

---

[15] Harry Levinson, *Organizational Diagnosis* (Cambridge, Mass.: Harvard University Press, 1972).

CHAPTER 3

Emotional Toxicity of the Work Environment

A SIMPLE WAY TO EXAMINE one's theoretical position and its useful-ness in a management context is to observe the manner in which managerial processes affect people. If we view man as an unfolding, maturing organism who, ideally, is actively interacting with his envi-ronment toward achieving his ego ideal while at the same time suc-cessfully managing his aggressive and sexual drives, his conscience or superego, and maintaining an effective relationship with his organiza-tion and his task, then we can readily observe those aspects of the work environment which inhibit his adaptation process. We can ob-serve the ways in which care and support are or are not provided by the organization, the presence or absence of institutional encourage-ment to growth, and the degree to which the organization allows a person to have an effect on his own fate. Such issues are more easily seen in the negative—that is, when they are absent or when adapta-tion is not successful—because, when these processes are working well, the smooth functioning of the organization makes it difficult for them to stand out in relief. Just as the physician learns more about the normal processes in the body from malfunction and illness, so any observer of the management scene will see a process magnified when he sees "pain" or dysfunction.

Seeing pain may throw a process into relief, but it may also con-tribute to a feeling of helplessness. It is of little help to me to hear a knock in the motor of my automobile if I cannot do something about it. Therefore, in addition to looking at psychological issues, in this chapter I would like to suggest various simple ways by which an executive or manager can cope with some of these issues. If the reader can see the nature of the problems with which he has to deal, and if he has some techniques he can apply that are in keeping with his managerial role and through which he can demonstrate to himself the validity of the frame of reference I am elaborating, he will be in a better position both to do his job more effectively and to give more careful consideration to other issues and problems as they are viewed from that same frame of reference.

To turn from the theory to implementation as a way of testing the theory, in this chapter I will address myself to the question of what the executive can do about recognizing and ameliorating some of the more obvious problems the organization creates for those who report to him.[1]

Imagine yourself two generations ago, when public health practitioners were urging people not to drink from the common drinking cup because it contained germs that carried disease. Imagine how difficult it must have been for people who had no concept of germs to understand that organisms existed that were invisible to the naked eye, let alone that could transmit disease. However, we have learned to accept the fact that there are microscopic agents that affect us, and we now give careful attention not only to bacteria, microbes, and viruses, but also to toxic agents such as gases. We can now make many infectious agents visible under the microscope. We now odorize or color gases. We no longer speak of magic or demons but point to real, concrete objects.

Despite what is known about the power of that which is not readily visible, management as a profession has not caught up altogether with other powerful nonvisible toxic agents, namely, feelings. It seems extremely difficult to grasp the idea that feelings are the primary precipitants of behavior and a major influence in health and sickness. Even today, in the face of a recent history of massive riots, social apathy, militant rebellion, and similar evidences of social disor-

---

[1] Two of my books spell out in greater detail many modes of executive action to deal with psychological issues: *Emotional Health: In the World of Work* (New York: Harper & Row, 1964); *Executive Stress* (New York: Harper & Row, 1970).

ganization, we still tend to think in terms of outside provocation rather than to ask: What do people feel? Why do they feel that way? How can something more positive be done about and with those feelings? The same is true when it comes to many physical illnesses that have important psychophysiological components. There is growing evidence to indicate that there are significant psychological components in coronary disease and even in cancer. By and large, however, management tends to avoid recognition of these powerful psychological forces.

He who would be concerned about how his organization affects people cannot avoid the impact of feelings on motivation and health. He must create for himself a psychological stethoscope to sense the feelings of his subordinates and must evolve means of keeping noxious feelings from inducing symptoms in individuals in the organization.

UNDERSTANDING THE FOUR FEELINGS

As I noted in the discussion on psychological man in Chapter 2, there are four major feelings with which every human being must deal: love, hate, feelings about dependency, and feelings about one's self-image.[2] Here I propose to elaborate them and suggest some ways in which the executive can sense them and do something about them.

Love

Every person needs to be able to give and to receive affection. Those who have difficulty loving other human beings invest themselves proportionately more in pets, causes, or hobbies. Some revel in the love of their spouses or their children, others in the affection of their dogs, and still others in the adulation of their followers. Whatever the case, it is necessary to give and to receive affection to survive, as studies of concentration camp survivors and the aged have confirmed.[3] The first question about any person whom an executive

---

[2] Levinson, *Emotional Health: In the World of Work.*

[3] Elmer Luchterhand, "Prisoner Behavior and Social System in the Nazi Concentration Camps," *The International Journal of Social Psychiatry*, XIII:4 (Autumn 1967), pp. 245–264. Marjorie F. Lowenthal and Clayton Haven, "Interaction and Adaptation: Intimacy as a Critical Variable," *American Sociological Review*, 33:1 (February 1968), pp. 20–30.

supervises, then, should be: "In what ways does he handle his need to give and to receive love and with what success?"

For example, some people need to be constantly applauded and encouraged. Others need to have the approval of their superiors but do not want to pay any attention to their subordinates. Still others keep their superiors at arm's length and seek the adulation of those who report to them. Some need the gratification which comes from pleasing customers. Others are involved with their work and could not care less about the people involved. Still others may deny in their behavior that they need anybody else's approval.

Hate

Konrad Lorenz demonstrated that aggression is an inborn animal instinct necessary for the survival of the species.[4] Freud theorized that this instinct to aggression becomes a psychological drive and is an important component of being able to act upon or master one's world. However, such a powerful drive that literally can result in someone else's death, a power necessary for self-defense and survival, can easily get out of hand. Hate, derived from aggression, is the most difficult of all feelings with which to deal. As Lorenz pointed out, and as cultural anthropologists have demonstrated in other ways, we set up elaborate mechanisms to transform aggression into constructive acts. We become guilty when we act in ways that seem to us destructively aggressive, even when those acts are merely symbolic, like telling somebody to go to hell. We are terribly frightened of being overwhelmed by our own aggressive impulses. Indeed, some people, such as catatonic schizophrenics, withdraw from the outside world for fear that they will destroy others. As every psychotherapist knows, the fear of one's own hostility leads to elaborate defensive mechanisms that cripple people psychologically. Often in desperation people turn their hostility on themselves, which can lead to suicide, accidents, self-inflicted injury, as well as self-defeat.[5]

The executive, therefore, should ask himself as he works with another person: How does this man handle his aggression? Is he able to

---

[4] Konrad Lorenz, *On Aggression* (New York: Harcourt Brace Jovanovich, 1966).

[5] K. A. Menninger, *Man Against Himself* (New York: Harcourt Brace Jovanovich, 1938).

channel it constructively and master it in constructive tasks? Does he displace it on other people? Does he contain it within himself so that various kinds of psychophysiological symptoms result? The key problem with aggression is the necessity for constructive channels for its discharge. Does he have them? Is more aggression being provoked than he can tolerate and is something being done about it? How can I, as an executive, decompress these feelings of hostility? Talking about it with him, suggesting outlets, and encouraging the man to confront the sources of his anger are some helpful ways. Discovering the ways he is frustrating others and providing him with more adequate modes of solving frustrating problems are even better ways.

For example, a man who is dealing with his anger by complaining to his subordinates or his peers might be encouraged to bring his angry feelings into discussion with his boss rather than to continue to handle them destructively through gossip. Some people manage their aggression by becoming ever more preoccupied with detail when under stress. The boss might well point out that there are more constructive ways than becoming immersed in detail; he might examine the intensity of the pressure he, the boss, is exerting, which may lead to that preoccupation. Some, in their angry frustration, pick on their subordinates. The boss can point out that destructive behavior and help the man learn to lead his subordinates to more effective problem solving. The boss might also ask whether his subordinate is merely imitating his own behavior. Some are unrealistic in their expectations of themselves and in their assumptions about how much responsibility they have. The boss can define what the responsibilities of the task are and are not.

Dependency

No human being can survive without being dependent on somebody else. For many people, however, to be a little dependent is the same as being totally dependent. This unconscious equation and the resultant negative feelings about dependency stem from the helplessness of infancy. The child strives to overcome his helplessness, to stand by himself, walk by himself, and be master of his own body and his own fate. None of us likes returning to a state of helplessness, and we fight vigorously against it. But all of us must come to terms with our dependency needs and evolve those situations for ourselves in relationships with companies, schools, hospitals, churches, and families which provide the most congenial mode of gratifying our dependency needs. Some people assert complete independence; others lean on the rest of the world all of the time.

The questions the executive should ask are: How does the man I am working with handle his dependency needs? How much dependency can he accept and how much must he reject? What supports for his dependency needs does he maintain and with what success? How much can he lean on his wife, his company, his children, his lodge? What role do I (the executive) play in this picture? How much can he count on his relationship with me? How do people in this organization expect it to support their dependency needs? Does it do so?

Dependency needs vary, depending on the problems people have to deal with. In crisis, people need much more support from their superiors. In a new situation, they need more frequent contact with superiors to help them get their bearings and establish momentum in the new job. In times of rapid change, they need much more information and guidance and greater strength of direction than in more stable periods. The more ambiguous a situation, the less it is structured, usually, the greater the need for discussion, mutual planning, and the spreading of risk about decision making.

Self-Esteem

Studies of the incidence and prevalence of mental and physical illness in industry indicate that the lower the person is in the organizational hierarchy, the more frequently and seriously he becomes ill. Analysis of the studies of mental health in industry indicates that these employees all touch on self-esteem as the central variable. As I have already noted, self-esteem is the distance between how one perceives himself to be—his self-image—and how he feels he ideally ought to be—his ego ideal. Failure to meet the demands of the ego ideal is one of the major sources of feelings of inadequacy. The lower the self-esteem, the greater the incidence of illness. The questions the executive should ask about his employees, then, are: What are their ego ideals? How do they ideally think they ought to be? How far do they feel from that? How worthless do they feel they are?

These questions are not easy to answer for one's self, let alone for others. There are a number of ways of getting partial answers. One way is to look at the choice points over a person's lifetime. When he had a choice between courses in school, what direction did he take? When he had career choices, what direction did he take? When he had task or job choices, what direction did he take? Although these may seem somewhat random, if one delineates the choice points and traces them out, he will observe a certain consistency to the choices that give thrust and direction to a person's life. Another way of ascertaining dimensions of the ego ideal is to ask who a person's heroes and models are or were. Still a third is to ask what were the peak experiences the person has had. Each of us in his lifetime has had one or two experiences during which he felt highly elated with himself. When one recalls those experiences and looks at his own behavior at those times, he may see in relief that state toward which he is striving. A critically important aspect of the ego ideal derives from the values of the parents. If a person can recall not so much what his parents did but how in behavior they emphasized certain values, he will probably then be able to discern more clearly (in his own ego) ideal elements of those values. Taken together, all of these modes of achieving the ego ideal will contribute to evolving a clearer definition. Certainly they provide a basis for thinking and discussion.

People often speak about the ego ideal when they talk about their expectations about promotion, about the quality of the work they like to do, and when they criticize themselves about how well they have done a given task. They reflect their negative feelings about themselves and their organization when they talk about how difficult it is to solve problems in the organization and how small the prospects seem for becoming effective in their problem-solving effort. Few people will say they feel worthless in a managerial situation, but they may express those feelings indirectly in the degree of pessimism or optimism with which they go about their efforts. Many organizations try to deal with such feelings by inspirational methods. But these rarely work for long because they provide no effective ways for a person to achieve gratification by successful problem solving to counter the underlying feelings of inadequacy.

RECOGNIZING THE SYMPTOMS

To turn to the work situation, whenever any of the four feelings are exacerbated by the organization, a person becomes ill. The symptoms may be physical, psychological, or both. There is no escape from the fact, however, that equilibrium will be altered.

Love

Whenever a person is deprived of his sources of affection in the work situation or of his opportunity to give his affection, the symptom, however subtle, will appear. Such losses occur if a person is removed from a congenial work group, if there is a change in the work process with which he is identified, if he is physically transferred to another community or moved to another section, if he is fired, or even if he is promoted; and there will be changes in his ability to attach himself to other people and to familiar and preferred objects. I shall discuss these issues in greater detail in Chapter 5. Suffice it to say here that in myriad ways we give and receive affection although often we do not regard our bantering with friends, our pride in task accomplishment, the ready availability of help from supervisors, peers, subordinates, and even organizational support from institutions, such as a medical department or a personnel department, as sources of affection.

Hate

Whenever anger is unnecessarily increased by unfair criticism, exploitation, poor planning, attack, or simply when a person is made to feel like an ass, the result will be some kind of symptom where people act against their own interests or those of the organization or both. Many managements have not learned that the unnecessary provocation of anger is destructive to them and to their people. Some still believe that, "You have to beat it out of them or you won't get production."

Dependency

Whenever people are made more dependent than they can allow themselves to be, when their natural human supports are undermined, when they cannot gratify their dependency needs, or when they are made to feel more helpless, then these frustrations will increase their anger. Some organizations undertake mistaken forms of paternalism in vain efforts to make their employees like them. Paternalism only increases the sense of dependency for the very word implies that the employer is a father and the employees are children. Such a relationship makes it impossible for people to see themselves as adults in their own eyes. In community rehabilitation efforts, for example, people insist on doing things themselves, because only if they solve their own problems and stand on their own feet can they be adults in their own eyes.

Self-Esteem

Whenever self-esteem is lowered by contempt or by arbitrary changes in a person's work patterns, work relationships, or his ability to be in charge of what's happening to him without having to consult with superiors, he inevitably feels he is being treated as a jackass. Lowered self-esteem stirs up anger within an individual and between himself and others. If he is conscientious and cannot sabotage the product or the organization, he will sabotage himself, which results in the increasing incidence of symptoms and illness. Sickness, absenteeism, and accidents must be viewed as withdrawal phenomena requiring investigation.

DEALING WITH THE PROBLEMS

The concerned executive will want to ask his people how their work is going for them and take the time to listen to what they say. He should ask himself what is happening to the four feelings for each person.

Love

What is happening to the ability to give and receive affection? If a man has lost his sources of affection, how can they be restored? The executive should encourage him to do something about it by, for example, making new friends, undertaking new activities, repairing old friendships, or even transferring to another group, if that is at all possible.

For example, a 42-year-old corporate vice president, newly promoted and transferred from a small midwestern town to New York City, complained of a range of vague, diffuse physical symptoms. Medical examination findings were essentially negative. A few minutes of conversation about how he was adjusting and how he liked what he was doing disclosed a lonely, unhappy man. He missed the camaraderie and affection of the small town. He did not see familiar faces on the street. His suburban community was as strange to him as a hotel room. He was a man who all his life had had close give-and-take relations with others. Now there were few with whom he could have that relationship. The opportunity to talk with the boss was his first chance to examine aloud the relationship between his psychological loss and the onset of his symptoms. At that point he could choose his own course of healing.

Hate

With respect to aggression, the executive should permit the person to ventilate his hostility and to get his anger out in the open. Once he has done so, he is in a better position to think about how he can cope with the provocations of the hostility he experiences. He can then examine his alternatives and find more constructive ways of handling his anger.

To illustrate, a 38-year-old vice president was specially selected for his post by the company president as his likely successor. However, the president played his own role close to his vest and used his chosen heir more as an office boy than as an officer. The younger man became increasingly angry. He tried to talk with his boss gently but could get nowhere. Thinking that perhaps he was not performing adequately, he asked for constructive criticism, but got none. He chafed and fumed, reluctant to leave and give up the opportunity to become head man in this company. He looked forward to a change of heart on the part of the president, eagerly sought ways to break through the latter's armor and to prove himself. Terribly frustrated as each effort failed, he finally took the opportunity to talk over his situation with someone outside the company. After he blew off steam, he came to recognize that the president had never been able to delegate authority, could not tolerate rivals, would not open up to him no matter what he did, and that he was, therefore, beating his head against a psychological wall. Now, he saw he could either wait for his turn patiently in the wings or go somewhere else.

Dependency

It is important for the executive to help a person understand that it is all right to be dependent on other people in varying degrees. We all are. We need to find ways of being independent from some, inter-dependent with others, and more heavily dependent on still others. Some people will need permission to be dependent, and so the executive, in effect, will have to give them that permission. Some people who demand very much of themselves cannot accept help from any-body without feeling an obligation. An understanding senior person can help such people find ways of helping somebody else, to repay the obligation they feel for being treated kindly or helpfully by oth-ers. Each person needs to know somebody needs him, each person needs to find somebody who does indeed need him. A colleague, friend, or boss can help him understand that and find ways of coping with his dependency needs more successfully.

A division manager for a public utility company was one of several such managers who were close to the vice president to whom they reported. The elder man was like a father to them and fostered each of his subordinate's careers. When the older man died, each felt the loss of his support. But this division manager resorted to alcohol. Only when he was required by his new boss to go to a physician could he begin to spill out his grief and loss. He, more than the oth-ers, needed a kindly father to lean on. The death of the older man made that apparent, but he dared not look for a substitute for that would be weakness. The physician talked with him several times, serving meanwhile as a temporary substitute, and helped him to see that each person has his own pattern of meeting his dependency needs, and that he need not be ashamed or embarrassed at recogniz-ing that he was a good No. 2 man. The manager's boss, recognizing his need for greater support, saw him more frequently in supervision.

Self-Esteem

A physician is often in the position of having to reassure his pa-tients that their bodies are all right, even that they are attractive bodies. An executive must often do the same with respect to the self-image of his employees. Sometimes the executive can point out to people that their ideals are impossible ones and their aspirations are but fantasies that no human being could achieve. He can sometimes also point out to people that their demands on themselves are too high, that they judge themselves too harshly and too unfairly, that they deprecate their achievements, and that they depreciate their assets. The executive may also have to reassure them that they are indeed doing well. This, in turn, will give them some relief from their self-demands and provide added strength to work more actively toward mastering their problems.

A hard-driving engineer described himself as so busy he had to take his lunch at his desk regularly. He talked about his long hours, late nights, and heavy responsibilities. When his boss asked him if he had to work that way and whether the company compelled or demanded it, he responded negatively. He felt he had to cover all bets, to be on top of every detail. He asked the boss how he compared with other young executives in the company. The boss reviewed his record of achievement with him and in effect made him demonstrate out loud to himself his competence and success. When he talked about his minor mistakes, the boss said, "Welcome to the human race." With some further efforts toward objectivity, the executive was able to help the young man relax somewhat and to see himself in a more accurate perspective.

CONCLUSION

My thesis is that there are four major feelings with which each one of us has to deal. These feelings can be exacerbated by what goes on in a work situation. The executive can help counteract the impact of these precipitants of negative stress by working with his juniors to help them understand that feelings are as powerful as germs, if not more so, and that feelings induce symptoms and illness that are just as severe as those produced by microbes or viruses. The executive who is unable to act in his organization to prevent illness can, nevertheless, understand the feelings his subordinates struggle with and how they approach them. He can then serve as a triangulating point, a point in reality against which the subordinate can mirror his feelings, look at them sometimes for the first time, understand that they are just as natural as other forms of infection and that he can combat them by undertaking counteracting activities. In such a case, the executive makes it possible for the person to really know those realities that are often most difficult to recognize, namely, feelings. Hope for a man is the fundamental ingredient of health. A man has emotional health when he knows what he is up against and has some effective ways of working at mastering the difficulty. If he neither knows what he is up against nor any way of mastering it, then he gives up. The task of the executive is to sustain hope and preserve vitality. To do that, he must be the agent of reality for his people and help them to see their own psychological microbes and the forces that cause them.

CHAPTER 4

On Being a Middle-Aged Manager

THE THESIS OF THIS BOOK is the conception of psychological man. Since psychological man is a heavily nativistic conception, one implication is that there are discernible stages in the process of growth and development. Not only must one understand these stages if he is to have a comprehensive grasp of motivation, but he must also understand the specific problems of managing internal and external factors that are unique to given stages, if he is to act reasonably and rationally with respect to motivation.

The concept of psychological man—a whole adaptive person maintaining an internal and external equilibrium—comes most vividly into view in relation to the issues of middle age. The crises of middle age have become increasingly the crises of executives. Crises of executives in turn become crises in organizations for they affect decision making, job performance, morale, and motivation. These crises relate, on the one hand, specifically to changes in the ego ideal with time and, on the other hand, to the nature of work and progress in organizations. These crises mobilize many feelings, including the crucial ones I have previously discussed. Negative exacerbation of these feelings is the core of executive stress. Executives must cope with them on behalf of themselves and the organizations for which they have responsibility.

For most men, attainment of executive rank coincides with the onset of middle age, that vast gulf that begins about the age of 35 and endures until a man has come to terms with himself and his human fate (for no man matures until he has done so). This period ex-

emplifies the peak of personal expansion, when a man lives most fully
the combined multiple dimensions of his life. He has acquired the
wisdom of experience and the perspective of maturity. His activity
and productivity are in full flower; his career is well along toward its
zenith. He is at the widest range of his travels and his contacts with
others. He is firmly embedded in a context of family, society, career,
and his own physical performance. His successes are models for emu-
lation; his failures, the object lessons for others. He has become a link
from the past to the future, from his family to the outside world,
from those for whom he is organizationally responsible to those to
whom he owes responsibility. In a word, he has it made.

And need it all come to a harsh and bitter end? *No.*

A man cannot alter his inevitable fate. But he can manage the way
he comes to terms with it. If he does so, rather than simply letting
events take their course, he can do much to prolong the richness of
his life as well as his years.

Sophocles, who lived to be more than 90, wrote *Oedipus Rex* at 75
and *Oedipus et Colonus* at 89. Titian completed his masterpiece, *The
Battle of Lepanto*, at 95; he began work on one of the most famous
paintings in the world, *The Descent from the Cross*, when he was 97.
Benjamin Franklin invented bifocals at 78. Benjamin Duggar, professor of plant physiology and botanical economics at the University of
Wisconsin, was removed at age 70 by compulsory retirement; he
then joined the research staff of Lederle Laboratories and several
years later gave mankind Aureomycin. Past 90, Pablo Casals still
plays the cello as no other man ever has. Santayana, the philosopher,
wrote his first novel, *The Last Puritan*, at 72. Carl Sandburg wrote
Remembrance Rock at 70. Freud's activities continued into his 80s.

These men are the exceptions, of course. But the fact that many
people can mature creatively indicates that there is indeed hope for
all of us who are closer to 35. In this chapter I propose to examine
some of the experiences of middle age and suggest ways of maintaining creative potential.

First, however, permit me a brief qualification. I am not splitting
men into arbitrary categories of under and over 35. That would be
unrealistic. The age of 35 is not fixed. It will be different for different
people because I am using it here in the sense of a stage of life, not a
birthday.

INDEXES OF HEALTH

Behind the flowering of middle age, a critical physical and psychological turnaround process is occurring. This is reflected in indexes of health. Statistics from Life Extension Examiners indicate that specific symptoms—such as extreme fatigue, indigestion, and chest pains—rise sharply among young executives just moving into top management. Only one-third of the symptoms found in the 31- to 40-year-old management group can be traced to an organic cause, the examiners report.[1] They suggest that these problems come about because of both the manner in which the men live and the state of mind in which they work.

Psychological Factors

While some explanations for that increase in symptoms are no doubt a product of the aging process itself, there are more pressing psychological forces. The British psychoanalyst, Elliott Jaques, contends that a peak in the death rate between 35 and 40 is attributable to the shock that follows the realization that one is inevitably on a descending path.[2] This produces what for most men is a transitory period of depression. Depression increases a person's vulnerability to illness. There is much medical evidence to indicate that physical illness is likely to occur more frequently and more severely in people who feel depressed.

Lee Stockford of the California Institute of Technology reports, from a survey of 1,100 men, that about 5 out of 6 men in professional and managerial positions undergo a period of frustration when they are in their middle 30s and that 1 man in 6 never fully recovers from it. Stockford attributes the crisis to a different kind of frustration: "This is the critical age—the mid-30s—when a man comes face to face with reality and finds that reality doesn't measure up to his dreams." [3]

A number of factors in executive life contribute to the intensification of these feelings and the symptoms that result.

---

[1] "Clinical Health Age: 30–40," *Business Week* (March 3, 1956), p. 56.

[2] Elliott Jaques, "Death and the Mid-Life Crisis," *The International Journal of Psychoanalysis* (October 1965), p. 502.

[3] Personal communication.

Increasing Contraction of the Hard-Work Period

The average age at which men become company presidents is decreasing. As it does, the age span during which success can be achieved becomes narrower. The competitive pace therefore becomes more intense. It is further intensified by devices such as management by objectives and performance appraisals which give added impetus to the pressures for profit objectives.

Inseparability of Life and Career Patterns

For managerial men in an intensely competitive career pattern, each year is a milepost. Time at a job or at a particular level is a critical variable. If one does not move along on time, he loses out on experience, position, and, above all, on the reputation for being a star. This means that there necessarily must be repetitive subpeaks of anxiety around time dimensions.

Continuous Threat of Defeat

When both internal and external pressures for achievement are so high, the pain of defeat—always harsh—can be devastating, no matter how well a man seems to take it. Animal research indicates that when males are paired in combat, up to 80 percent of the defeated ones subsequently die, although their physical wounds are rarely severe enough to cause death. We cannot generalize from animals to humans, but we can get some suggestion of the physical cost of the experience of personal defeat. When we turn back to the management pyramid and the choices that have to be made, obviously many men experience defeat, and all must live with the threat.

Increase in Dependency

To cope with competition, the executive, despite his misgivings, must depend on specialists whose word he has to accept because of his lack of specialized knowledge. In fact, John Kenneth Galbraith advanced the thesis in *The New Industrial State* that the technical infrastructure of an organization really makes the decisions, leaving only pro forma approval for the executive.[4] The specialists have their

---

[4] John Kenneth Galbraith, *The New Industrial State* (Boston: Houghton Mifflin, 1967).

own concepts, jargon, and motivation, which often differ from those of the executive. Every executive wants to make good decisions. He is uneasy about decisions based on data he does not fully understand, gathered by people he does not fully understand, and presented in terms he does not fully understand. He is, therefore, often left to shudder at the specter of catastrophe beyond his control.

Denial of Feelings

Commitment to executive career goals requires self-demand and self-sacrifice, while simultaneously inhibiting close, affectionate relationships. One cannot allow himself to get close to those with whom he competes or about whom he must make decisions or who are likely to make decisions about him. Often he bears a burden of guilt for the decisions he must make about the careers of others.[5] No matter how strongly a man wants the achievement goals, he still has some feelings of anger, toward both himself and the organization that demands that sacrifice, for having to give up other desirable life goals. He must hold in tightly these feelings of anger, together with the feelings of affection and guilt, if they are unacceptable to him or to his business culture. Repressed feelings must be controlled continuously, a process that requires hyper-alertness and, therefore, energy.

Constant State of Defensiveness

The pursuit of executive success is like playing the children's game, King of the Hill. In that game, each boy is vying for the place at the top of the stump, fence, barrel, or even, literally, the hill. All the others try to push the incumbent from his summit perch. Unlike the game, in executive life there is no respite. Given this state of affairs, together with the other conditions to which I have just referred, one must always be "at the ready," as the military put it. To be at the ready psychologically means that one's whole body is in a continuing emergency state, with resulting greater internal wear and tear.

Shift in the Prime-of-Life Concept

Western societies value youth. It is painfully disappointing to have attained a peak life stage at a time in history when that achievement

---

[5] See Harry Levinson, *Emotional Health: In the World of Work* (New York: Harper & Row, 1964), Chapter 18.

is partially vitiated by worship of youth, when there is no longer as much respect for age or seniority. This is compounded by one's awareness of the decline of his physical capacities. Thus, at the height of a manager's attainment, he is likely to feel also that he has only partly made it, that he has already lost part of what he sought to win. Since only rarely can one have youth and achievement at the same time, there is something anticlimactic about middle-aged success.

SUBTLE CHANGES

The issues having to do with health are only one facet of the middle-aging process. There are also subtle, but highly significant, changes in (1) work style, (2) point of view, (3) family relationships, and (4) personal goals. Let us look at each of these in turn.

Work Style

Both the mode and the content of the work of creative men differ in early adulthood, or the pre–35-year stage, from that of mature adulthood, or the post–35-year stage. Jaques pointed this out when he observed:

> The creativity of the 20s and early 30s tends to be a hot-from-the-fire creativity. It is intense and spontaneous, and comes out ready-made. . . . Most of the work seems to go on unconsciously. The conscious production is rapid, the pace of creation often being dictated by the limits of the artist's capacity physically to record the words or music he is expressing. . . . By contrast, the creativity of the late 30s and after is sculptured creativity. The inspiration may be hot and intense. The unconscious work is no less than before. But there is a big step between the first effusion of inspiration and the finished creative product. The inspiration itself may come more slowly. Even if there are sudden bursts of inspiration they are only the beginning of the work process.[6]

Jaques adds that the inspiration for the older man is followed by a period of forming and fashioning the product, working and reworking the material, and acting and reacting to what he has formed. This is an experience that may go on for years. The content of work

---

[6] Jaques, "Death and the Mid-Life Crisis," p. 503.

changes, too, from a lyrical or descriptive content to one that is tragic and philosophical, followed by one that is serene. Jaques recalls that Shakespeare wrote his early historical plays and comedies before he was 35, his tragedies afterward.

Contrary to popular belief, creativity does not cease at an early age. It is true that creative men have made major contributions before they were 40, but it is equally true that those who demonstrated such creativity continued to produce for many years thereafter. In fact, both in the arts and in the sciences, the highest output occurs when men are in their 40s.

Executives have many of the same kinds of experiences as artists and scientists. Executives report the greatest self-confidence at 40. Though their instrumentality is the organization, younger and older men do different creative work with organizations. The younger man is more impulsive, flashy, and starbright with ideas; the older man is more often concerned with building and forming an organization. A conspicuous example is the hard-hitting company founder who, to the surprise of his organization, becomes less concerned with making money and more preoccupied with leaving an enduring company. Suddenly, he is talking about management development.

Point of View

Concurrent with the shift in work style or orientation is a shift in point of view. This occurs in political and social thinking as well as in business. It is a commonplace that most people become more conservative as they grow older. It is an unspoken commonplace that they are more bored.

True, many activities are intrinsically boring and become more so with repetition, but others no longer hold interest when one's point of view has changed.

Disillusionment. Some of the boredom results from disillusionment. Early idealism, the tendency toward action, and the conviction of the innate goodness in people are in part a denial of the inevitable. Young people in effect say, "The world can be rosy. I'll help make it that way. People can be good to each other if only someone will show them how or remove the conditions that cause their frustration."

But in mid-life it becomes clear that people are not always good to each other; that removing the conditions of frustration does not always lead to good, friendly, loving behavior; and that people also have a capacity for being ugly and self-destructive. One evidence for the denial of disillusionment is the effort in so many companies to keep things "nice and quiet." Such companies are characterized by the inability to accept conflict as a given and conflict resolution as a major part of the executive's job.

Obsolescence. Another factor in change in point of view has to do with the feeling of becoming increasingly obsolescent. The middle-aged man feels himself to be in a world apart from the young— emotionally, socially, and occupationally. This is covered today by the cliché "generation gap." But there is something real to that distance because there is a tendency to feel that one cannot keep up with the world no matter how fast he runs. Thus the sense of incompetence, even helplessness, is magnified. Some of this is reflected in an attitude that middle-aged executives often take.

For example, I once addressed the 125 members of the upper management group of a large company. When I finished, I asked them to consider three questions in the discussion groups into which they were going to divide themselves:

(1) Of what I had said, what was most relevant to their business?
(2) Of what was most relevant, what order of priority ought to be established?
(3) Once priority was established, who was to do what about the issues?

They handled the first question well when they reported back; none had difficulty specifying the relevant. They had a little more difficulty with the second. None touched the third; it was as if they felt they were not capable of taking the action with which they had been charged.

Vocational Choice. That incident might be excused on a number of bases, if it were not for other unrelated or corroborative evidence that reflects a third dimension in our consideration of change in point of view. Psychologist Anne Roe did a series of studies on vocational choice in the adult years. In one study she was trying to find out how people make decisions about selecting jobs. She reports that

the most impressive thing about these interviews was how few of our subjects thought of themselves as considering alternatives and making decisions based on thoughtful examination of the situation. . . . They seemed not to recognize their role as chooser or their responsibility for choices. It was, indeed, this last aspect we found most depressing. Even among the executives, we find stress on contingencies and external influences more often than not.[7]

Pain of Rivalry. The sense of being more distant from the sources of change, from the more impulsive agents of change, and of not being a chooser of one's fate spawns feelings of helplessness and inadequacy. This sense of remoteness is further magnified, as I have already noted, by feelings of rivalry. For boys, playing King of the Hill may be fun. For men, the greater the stakes and the more intense the motivation to hold one's place, the more threatening the rivals become. Yet, in the midst of this competitive environment, one is required to prepare his rivals to succeed him and ultimately to give way. The very name of the game is Prepare Your Successor.

I recall a particular corporate situation in which the president had to decide who was to be executive vice president. When he made his choice, some of his subordinates were surprised because, they said, the man he picked was the hottest competitor for the president's job and usually such men were sabotaged. The surprising part of the event, as far as I was concerned, was not the choice but the fact that the subordinates themselves had so clearly seen what tends to happen to rivals for the executive suite. It is indeed difficult to tolerate a subordinate when the executive senses himself to be, in any respect, on a downward trail while the subordinate is obviously still on his way up and just as obviously demanding his place in the corporate sun.

This phenomenon is one of the great undiscussed dilemmas of the managerial role. Repeatedly, in seminars on psychological aspects of management, cases refer to executives who cannot develop others, particularly men that have nothing to fear, in the sense that their future security is assured and they still have upward avenues open to them. What is not seen, let alone understood, in such cases is the terrible pain of rivalry in middle age in a competitive business context that places a premium on youth. This paragraph from Budd

---

[7] Anne Roe and Rhoda Baruch, "Occupational Changes in the Adult Years," *Personnel Administration* (July–August 1967), p. 32.

Schulberg's *Life* review of *Thalberg: Life and Legend* captures the rivalry issue in one pointed vignette:

> There was to be a dramatic coda to the Irving Thalberg Story: the inevitable power struggle between the benevolent but jealous L. B. Mayer and the protégé he "loved like a son." Bitter was the conflict between Father and Son fighting over the studio's Holy Ghost. They fought over artistic decisions. They fought over separation of authorities. They fought over their division of the spoils, merely a symbol of power, for by now both were multimillionaires. It was as if the old, tough, crafty beachmaster L. B. was determined to drive off the young, frail but stubborn challenger who dared ask Mayer for an equal piece of the billion-dollar action.[8]

In that case, the rivalry was visible in open conflict. It could be with men at that level and in that culture. However, in most cases, if the rivalry does not go on unconsciously, it is carefully disguised and rationalized. Executives are reluctant to admit such feelings even to themselves. Therefore, much of the rivalry is unconscious. The parties are less aware of why they are quarreling, or perhaps they are more aware of the fact that they never seem to settle their quarrels. Every executive can test such feelings in his own experience by reviewing how he felt when a successor took his place, even though he himself moved up, particularly when that successor changed some of his cherished innovations.

Thus it is difficult for each of us to see the unconscious battle he wages with subordinates, now wanting them to succeed, now damned if they will. Subordinates, however unable they are to see this phenomenon in themselves, can usually see it quite clearly in the behavior of the boss or superior. But then there are few upward performance appraisals to help make such behavior conscious, and the behavior itself indicates to the subordinate that the rival would do well to keep his mouth shut.

Dose of Anger. The change in point of view that throws such problems into relief and intensifies fear (though rarely do executives speak of fear) is compounded further by a significant dose of anger. It

---

[8] Budd Schulberg, "Book Review: *Thalberg: Life and Legend,*" *Life* (February 28, 1969), p. 6.

is easy to observe the anger of the middle-aged executive toward to-day's youth—who have more money, more opportunity, and more sex than was available yesterday. There is anger, too, that the young-sters are free to "do their thing" while today's executives, pressed by the experiences of the depression and the constraints of their positions, sometimes find it hard to do what they really want to do.

The anger with youth is most often expressed as resentment because "they want to start at the top" or "they aren't willing to wait their turn or get experience" or "they only want young ones around here now." It is further reflected in such simultaneously pejorative and admiring descriptive nouns as "whiz kids," "jets," and "stars." These mixed-feeling phrases bespeak self-criticism and betrayal.

Every time the middle-aged manager uses such a phrase, he seems also to be saying that he has not done as well or that he has been undercut. He who had to learn how to size up the market from firsthand contact with customers finds that knowledge now useless; computer models constructed by a man who never canvassed a customer are increasingly in use. He who thought business to be "practical" and "hardheaded" now finds that he must go back to school, become more intellectual, think ahead conceptually, or he is lost. The kids have outflanked him. They have it so good, handed to them on a platter, at his expense.

Older generations have always complained that the youth not only are unappreciative of their elders' efforts but take for granted what they have struggled so hard to achieve. Nevertheless, management has never taken seriously the impact of such feelings on executive behavior. The result is an expensive loss of talent as it becomes apparent to young people that managements promise them far more than companies deliver.

I am certain in my own mind that it is the combination of rivalry and anger which makes it so difficult to create challenging ways to use young people in management. (Certainly it is not the dearth of problems to be tackled.) That in turn accounts for much of the astronomical turnover of young college graduates in their first years in a company and also for much of their subsequent disillusionment with managerial careers.

Family Relationships

The same narrowing that occurs in the cycle of achievement in business has also been taking place within the family. People are marrying at earlier ages and children are being born earlier in the marriage and, therefore, leaving their parents earlier. In turn, the parents live alone with each other longer (according to latest census figures, an average of 16 years). This poses several problems that come to a head in middle life. By this point in time one usually has lost both his parents. Though he may have been independent for many years, nevertheless for the first time he feels psychologically alone.

Because an executive can less readily establish close friendships at work and because his mobility makes it difficult for him to sustain them in his off-work relationships, he tends to have greater attachment to his children. He therefore suffers greater loss when they leave home, and he usually does not compensate for these losses any more than he actively compensates for the loss of old friendships through death and distance.

His heavy commitment to his career and his wife's to the children tend to separate them from each other—a problem that is obscured while their joint focus is on the children. When the children leave home, he is left with the same conscious reasons for which he married her as the basis for the marriage (attractiveness, charm, liveliness), and often the same unconscious ones (a substitute for mother, anything but like mother, a guaranteed nonequal, and other, similarly unflattering, reasons). But she is no longer the young girl he married. She has aged, too, and is probably no longer her ideal sylph-like self of 20 years before. If, in addition, his unconscious reasons for marrying her are now no longer as important as they were earlier, there is little left for the marriage unless the couple has worked out bases for mutual usefulness.

Meanwhile, for most couples there has been a general decrease in satisfaction with each other, less intimacy, a decline in frequency of sexual intercourse, and fewer shared activities. Wives become more preoccupied with their husbands' health because age compels them to unconsciously rehearse for widowhood. Husbands sense this concern and the reasons (which sometimes include a wish for widowhood) for it, and withdraw even more. This is part of what increases the sense of loneliness mentioned earlier, in the context of the need for greater closeness. These factors contribute to the relatively new phenomenon of the "20-year" divorce peak.

Personal Goals

Up to approximately age 45, creative executive effort is largely self-centered. That is, one is concerned with his achievement and his personal needs. After age 45, the executive gradually turns to matters outside himself. As psychologist Else Frenkel-Brunswik has shown, he becomes more concerned with ideals and causes, derived from religious or parental values.[9] He also becomes more concerned with finding a purpose in life.

For example, a young executive, a "jet" in his company, became a subsidiary president early in his career. And while in that role he became involved in resolving racial problems in his community. Although still president, and likely to be promoted to head the whole corporation, his heart is now in the resolution of community problems. Similarly, another executive has retired early to become involved in conservation. Still others leave business for politics, and not a few have become Episcopal priests.

As part of this change (which goes on unconsciously), there are periods of restlessness and discomfort. There appears to be a peak in travel between the ages of 45 and 50 and also a transitory period of loneliness as one leaves old, long-standing moorings, and seeks others.

The restlessness and discomfort have another source. When the middle-aged manager is shifting his direction, he must necessarily use psychological energy for that task. As a consequence, it is more difficult to keep ancient, repressed conflicts under control. This is particularly true when the manager has managed to keep certain conflicts in check by promising himself he would one day deal with them. As he begins to feel that time is running out and that he has not delivered on his promises to himself, he begins to experience in-

<hr>

[9] Else Frenkel-Brunswik, "Adjustments and Reorientation in the Course of the Life Span," in Bernice L. Neugarten, ed., *Middle Age and Aging* (Chicago: The University of Chicago Press, 1968), p. 81.

tense internal frustration and pressure. Sometimes he will try to hide such conflicts under a contemporary slogan such as "identity crisis."

Not long ago, a 42-year-old executive told me that, despite his age, his professional engineering training, and his good position, he was still having an identity problem. He said he really did not know what he wanted to do or be. A few questions quickly revealed that he would prefer to be in his own business. However, the moment we touched that topic, he was full of excuses and wanted to turn away from it. He did indeed know what he wanted to do; he was simply afraid to face it. He wanted to be independent but he could not break away from the security of his company. He had maintained the fantasy that he might some day, but as the passing years made that less likely, his conflict increased in intensity.

Most men will come nowhere near doing all they want to do with their lives. All of us have some degree of difficulty and frustration as a result. We become even more angry with ourselves when we begin to realize that time will run out before we have sampled, let alone savored, much of what there is in the world. But most of us subtly turn our efforts to meeting those ideal requirements.

The important point in all this is that, as psychologist Charlotte Buhler points out, it relates directly to survival.[10] The evidence indicates that a person's assessment about whether he did or did not reach fulfillment has more to do with his old-age adjustment than with the literal loss of physical capacities and insecurity. Put another way, if a man has met his own standards and expectations reasonably well, he adapts more successfully to the aging process. If not, the converse holds: while experiencing the debilitation of aging, he is also simultaneously angry with himself for not having done what he should have. Anger with self is the feeling of depression. And I have already noted the implications of depression on physical illness.

SIGNIFICANT IMPLICATIONS

Up to this point, I have been discussing the critical physical and

---

[10] Charlotte Buhler, quoted by Raymond G. Kuhlen in "Developmental Changes in Motivation During the Adult Years," in Bernice L. Neugarten, ed., *Middle Age and Aging*, p. 134.

psychological symptoms of the aging process. Now I shall turn to the personal and organizational implications in all this.

Facing the Crisis

First, all of us must face up to the fact that there is such an event in a man's life as middle-aged crisis. It is commonplace; it need not be hidden or apologized for. It frequently takes the form of depressive feelings and psychosomatic symptoms and increased irritability and discontent, followed by declining interest in and efforts toward mastering the world.

There is a premature tendency to give in to fate, to feel that one can have no choice about what happens to him and, in effect, to resign oneself to the vagaries of chance. This period is essentially a mourning experience: regret, sorrow, anger, disappointment for something that has been lost—one's precious youth—and with it the illusion of omnipotence and immortality. It is necessary to be free to talk about the loss, the pain, and the regret and even to shed a tear, literally or figuratively. We do indeed die a bit each day; we have a right to be shaken by the realization when we can no longer deny it.

When a middle-aged manager begins to experience such feelings, and particularly if they begin to interfere with his work or his enjoyment of life, he should talk to someone else about them, preferably a good counselor. This kind of mourning is far better than increasing the intense pace of running in an effort to escape reality. In the process of talking, the wise man reworks his life experiences and his feelings until he is all mourned out and no longer afraid of being mortal.

When a manager can take his own life transitions and his feelings about them seriously, he has achieved the beginnings of maturity. In the course of making wine, after the grapes are pressed, the resulting liquid is left to age. In a sense, it continues to "work." In the process of aging, it acquires body, color, and bouquet—in short, its character.

As with wine, people who work over their feelings about the aging process acquire a certain character with age. They deepen their awareness of themselves and others. They see the world in sharper perspective and with greater tolerance. They acquire wisdom. They love more, exploit less. They accept their own imperfections and therefore their own contributions. As Jaques has put it, "The successful outcome of mature creative work lies thus in constructive resignation both to the imperfections of men and to shortcomings in one's work. It is this constructive resignation which then imparts serenity to life and work." [11]

The middle-aged manager who fails to take himself, his crises, and his feelings seriously keeps running, intensifies his exploitation of others, or gives up to exist on a plateau. Some managers bury themselves more deeply in their work, some run after their lost youth with vain cosmetic efforts, others chase women, and still others pursue more power. A man's failure to mature in this sense then becomes a disease that afflicts his organization. He loses his people, his grasp of the realities of his life, and can only look back on the way it used to be as the ideal.

The executive who denies his age in these ways also denies himself the opportunity to prepare for what is to come, following some of the suggestions I shall discuss in the next section. He who continues to deny and to run will ultimately have to face emptiness when he can no longer do either and must still live with himself. The wise man will come to terms with reality early: he will take seriously the fact that his time is limited.

Taking Constructive Action

Second, a man must act. Only he who acts on his own behalf is the master of himself and his environment. Too many people accept what is for what will be. They most often say, "I can't do anything about it." What they really mean is that they won't do anything. Check your own experience. How often do you mean "won't" when you say "can't"? Much of psychotherapeutic effort is directed toward helping people see how they have trapped themselves this way. There are indeed alternatives in most situations. Our traps are largely self-made.

There are a number of fruitful avenues for action in both personal and business life. In personal terms, the most important efforts are the renegotiation of the marriage and the negotiation of new friendships. Husband and wife might wisely talk out their accumulated differences, their disappointments and mutual frustrations, and their

---

[11] Jaques, "Death and the Mid-Life Crisis," p. 505.

wishes and aspirations. As they redefine their marriage contract, they clarify for themselves their interdependence or lack of it. If they remain silent with each other or lash out in their frustration, they run the danger of destroying the marriage or falling apart themselves in their anger at the expense of their need for each other.

In social terms, the executive must make a formal effort to find and cultivate new friends with a particular emphasis on developing companionship. We know from studies of concentration camp survivors and of the process of aging that those who have companions cope most effectively with the traumas of life. Those who do not almost literally die of their loneliness. As a man becomes less self-centered, he can devote more energy to cultivating relationships with other people. When he individualizes and cultivates the next person, he creates the conditions for others' recognition of him as a person.

In public terms, the executive must become future oriented but this time in conceptions that go beyond himself and his job. He invests himself in the future when he becomes actively involved in some on-going activity of social value that has enduring purpose. Hundreds of schools, colleges, hospitals, and community projects—most of them obscure—await the capable man who gives a damn and wants that damn to matter. Most executives need not look more than a few blocks beyond their offices for such opportunities.

In business terms, the executive should recognize that at this point in time he ideally should be exercising a different kind of leadership and dealing with different organization problems. In middle age—the stage Erik Erikson has called "the period of generativity," [12]—if he opts for wisdom, he becomes an organizational resource for the development of others. His wisdom and judgment give body to the creative efforts of younger men. They help to turn impulse into reality and then to shape and reshape it into a thousand useful products and services. The executive thus acquires those characteristics that are to be admired and emulated. He shifts from quarterback to coach, from day-to-day operations to long-range planning. He becomes more consciously concerned with what he is going to leave behind him.

---

[12] Erik Erikson, *Childhood and Society* (New York: W. W. Norton, 1964), p. 13.

Organizing for Renaissance

Third, organizations must take the middle-aged period seriously in their thinking, planning, and programming. I know of no organization—business, university, church, or hospital—that does. No one knows how much effectiveness is lost.

If one of the needs for coping with middle-aged stress is the opportunity to talk about it, then part of every supervisory and appraisal counseling should be devoted to some of the issues and concerns of this state. Company physicians or medical examining centers should provide time for the patient to talk with the doctor about the psychological aspects of his age and his life. Sessions devoted to examining how groups are working together should, if they are middle-aged groups, have this topic on the agenda. Company educational programs should inform both men and their wives about this period and its unique pressures. Personnel counselors should give explicit attention to this issue in their discussions.

Obviously, there should be a different slant to executive or managerial training programs for men over 35 than for those under 35. Programs for those under 35 should be geared to keeping the younger men "loose." They should be encouraged to bubble, to tackle old problems afresh. This is not the time to indoctrinate men with rules and procedures but, rather, to stimulate them toward their own horizons. Training challenges should be around tasks requiring sparkle, flashes of insight, and impulsive action.

Developmental programs for men over 35 should be concentrated largely on retraining, updating, and conceptualizing the problems and the organization. Tasks and problems requiring reorganization, reformulation, refining, and restructuring are tasks for men whose psychological time it is to rework. Brilliant innovative departures are unlikely to come from such men, except as they are the fruition of a lifetime of ferment, as was the *aggiornamento* of Pope John XXIII.

For them, instead, more attention should be given to frequent respites from daily organizational chores to get new views, to examine and digest them in work groups, and to think of their application to organizational problems and issues. When they move toward the future, they are likely to go in protected steps, like the man crawling on ice who pushes a plank before him. Pushing them hard to free themselves of the plank will tend to paralyze them. Rather, training programs should specifically include small experimental attempts to apply new skills and views with minimum risk.

Much of managerial training for these men should be focused on how to rear younger men. This means not only emphasis on coaching, counseling, teaching, and supporting, but also time and opportunity to talk about their feelings of rivalry and disappointment, to ventilate their anger at the young men who "have it so good." Finally, these training programs should include the opportunity for the older men to recognize, understand, and accept their uniquely human role. Instead of rejecting the younger men, they can then more comfortably place their bets and cheer their favorites on. In the youngsters' winning, they, too, can win.

For the executive, his subordinates, and the company, middle age can truly be a renaissance.

CHAPTER 5

On the Experience of Loss

THE MATURATIONAL PROCESS, ideally a step-by-step evolution of continuous growth and integration, is frequently undermined by events which either undo some of the steps that have been taken or which inhibit the taking of further steps. In this chapter, I shall take a look at that most pervasive phenomenon that does both, namely, the experience of loss. It is when one must deal with such issues that he sees the most crucial difference between such conceptions as social man and self-actualizing man, on the one hand, and psychological man on the other. Earlier theories offer the executive little to increase his perception and awareness of such problems. However, with such perception and awareness, the executive can move to avoid impairment or to compensate, both in his own life and that of others in his organization, for the consequences of the loss experience.

WHAT IS THE EXPERIENCE OF LOSS?

Loss is a universal problem and probably the most psychologically costly one. It is the psychological experience underlying alienation, rootlessness, and the severe stresses of the family. Those terms and phrases—alienation, transiency and the stresses of the family—are short descriptive capsules that encompass complex and subtle processes. However, they say little about the underlying psychological loss experience on which they are based or how to cope with this loss. In the process of addressing that underlying psychological experience in this chapter, I shall take up three questions:

(1) Why is this experience so significant and how does it have its effects?

(2) What implications does the significance of this experience have for the manager and his family?

(3) What implications does it have for organizational practices, particularly those relating to people?

The reason the loss experience is so powerfully destructive can be seen in a simple analogy.

Imagine a tree rooted in the ground. The roots serve not only as a transmission route for nourishment but they also give the tree stability against the elements. When any of these roots is destroyed, some of its leaves begin to wither; some of the tree dies. If the tree is to be moved, a wise tree mover will cut away some of the more extended roots on one side of the tree, allow the tree time to adapt to that loss by developing new roots, then cut away some on the other side of the tree, leaving a large ball of dirt in which the remaining roots, including the newly proliferated ones, are contained. The human experience is much like that of the tree. We attach ourselves to other people, places, things, goals, wishes, aspirations, skills, knowledge and even life styles.

The experience of loss is the reaction to the destruction of attachments. It includes mixed feelings of deprivation, helplessness, sorrow, and anger in varying degrees. Deprivation of different kinds of psychological nourishment constitutes the essence of the loss experience. Among the most critical are: (1) loss of love, (2) loss of support, (3) loss of sensory input, and (4) loss of the capacity to act on oneself or the outside world.

Loss of love is easy to understand when a relative or a close friend dies. In the business world, being removed from one's old friends or business associates on whom one has depended for certain skills and competences and exchanges of information is an example. The separation from a highly valued business partner or colleague sometimes may be equally as painful as separation or divorce from a spouse. Movement within or out of an organization where important sources of regard and approval are left behind are other examples.

The second kind of loss, loss of support, occurs in the same three areas—close personal relationships, moving, and career changes—

when one has to establish new ties or relationships, find new people to depend upon, and adopt new ways of doing things. This is one of the reasons why many people are confused in new situations, even when the new situation is a long-sought-for advancement. Loss of support also occurs when a man can no longer use once-valued skills, practices, or theories, particularly if he depended on them for his self-esteem. This is one of the major reasons why new advances are not adopted in business practice.

The loss of sensory input occurs when people find it difficult to get the kind of data they need to protect and orient themselves. When people are in new situations as a result of being promoted, demoted, or reassigned, or when they have moved to a new city, they usually require some time to pick up significant cues about how to behave in a given location. This is particularly evident when people do not have the language facility or the familiarity with customs that the new place or new situation requires.

Finally, when, for whatever reasons, we feel more dependent on others and less able to act to solve our own problems, we are less the masters of ourselves and our own fates. We don't like our incomplete, less adequate selves. The consequence is that we feel more helpless and, therefore, probably more frightened, more vulnerable, more defensive, more frustrated, more angry, and more depressed. This is seen most often when reorganizations take place, in mergers, and in the installation of new technical or managerial processes.

The effects of loss are conspicuous in organizations. Certainly much of what is viewed as remaining on an organizational plateau, becoming organizational deadwood, or losing interest in one's job, even much of what is referred to laughingly as having risen to a level of incompetence,[1] results from the burden of depression due to the sense of loss. The import of the loss experience for management goes beyond these common experiences. It is encapsulated in three axioms:

> (1) All change is loss. Promotion, transfer, demotion, reorganization, merger, retirement, and most other managerial actions produce

---

[1] Laurence J. Peter and Raymond Hull, *Peter Principle: Why Things Always Go Wrong* (New York: Morrow, 1969).

change. Despite the fact that change is necessary and often for the better, the new always displaces the old and, at some level of consciousness, loss is experienced.

(2) There is evidence to indicate that losses, particularly if they are chronic and are accompanied by a sense of hopelessness, precipitate major illness, including life-threatening maladies.[2] All losses have important psychological and physiological significance. Extreme examples related to work include long-term unemployment or the inability to change or escape oppressive conditions of work. Less striking examples are the symptoms that arise when the plant itself is moved or when there are significant changes in the way work is done, as in automating work processes.

(3) Moreover, when not inhibited from doing so, people automatically begin a restitution process to recoup their losses and compensate for them. And the manager, with little more effort than it takes to ignore the effects of loss, can become a facilitator of the restitutive process. Thus he is in a position to be both an agent of prevention and a healer while, at the same time, carrying out his managerial role more effectively.

CORPORATE IMPLICATIONS

With respect to people who work in organizations, loss experiences range clearly along the four dimensions discussed in the preceding section.

Loss of Love

People experience loss of love when the organization changes its ways of treating its people so that they feel less valued. Such experiences may range from the extreme of closing a plant to breaking up familiar work relationships, as in restructuring the organization; to changing product mix so that those who made previously highly valued products are now no longer in a favored position; to industrial engineering speedup activities that make people feel that "it's only a place to work." Any action that decreases the feeling in a man of being valued as a person is a powerful precipitant of the feeling of loss of love and usually produces behavioral consequences such as anger and resistance as well as more subtle psychological and physiological reactions, like anxiety and illness.

---

[2] Thomas Holmes and Minoru Masuda, "Symposium on Separation and Depression," American Association for the Advancement of Science, December 1970.

Loss of Support

Loss of support takes many different forms, ranging from being separated from key people who were helpful to a person, to losing familiar ways of getting the job accomplished that are peculiar to a given situation, to the loss of opportunity for favored ways of behaving. For example, a man who knows his way around a company, who is intimately familiar with its politics and operates comfortably behind the scenes, will find himself at a considerable disadvantage in another part of the organization where he does not know his way around politically and where he has to operate out in the open. The characteristically active man will find himself at a loss in a situation where he must more often remain passive. By the same token, less competitive people will find themselves to have lost their favored ways of behaving when they are required to be more competitive. We see much of the latter phenomenon in contemporary business as historically staid businesses seek to become more aggressive.

A more subtle form of loss of support is usually glossed over by managers. People who have identified with an organization's purposes, goals, and leadership feel they have lost something when any of those change. For example, a retail establishment that prided itself on its reputation for service and high-quality merchandise and saw itself as a leader in its field and in its community was merged into a chain. The employees became demoralized because they were no longer able to take the time to serve their customers as well as they had before the merger. Problems in service and delivery mounted. The store lost its dominant local leadership, good employees began to leave, and others marked time as best they could.

Implicit in the loss of organizational identification is the loss of opportunity for a man to work toward his personal ego ideal, that image of himself at his future best (everyone's internalized criterion of personal success). When people can no longer feel that they are working successfully at being good and becoming better, they will often become frustrated and depressed and feel, concomitantly, utterly worthless, no matter what they have achieved up to that point. The same phenomenon occurs in a different way for managers who have achieved positions they had desired for a long time; that is, they have "made it." This happens to people who have reached their end-point position in the hierarchy or who have made their own businesses successful or who have become bored by doing the same thing repetitively. They begin to ask, "What next?" or "What do you do after you have it made?" or "Where do I go from here?" Such men show how powerful and threatening the loss experience can be when they refuse to train successors or to yield their organizations to successors.

A similar phenomenon occurs when a man has moved up in the company hierarchy and taken with him those people with whom he has learned to work well and on whom he depends heavily. If the time comes when he can no longer be surrounded by his loyal followers, or when he must retire, those who have risen with him are devoid of what gave them organizational interest and purpose. They then experience severe loss, particularly if they themselves never expected to rise to the top. Usually they are left to regret and to mourn despite their high positions.

Loss of Sensory Input

Loss of sensory input means essentially that one no longer gets that kind of information which helps him to orient himself in time and place. It may not be the absence of information per se but a person's inability to sense it. For example, it is of no help to a person to read a computer printout if he has not had the training to understand it. Similarly, a man promoted from the ranks to a supervisory or managerial role frequently loses the ability to learn what is going on among his subordinates unless he has had training in how to conduct meetings and to talk with people who have less power than he. A man who is accustomed to understanding what goes on in the plant merely by hearing the typical plant noises, when moved into another role will feel very uneasy about what may be going wrong because he can no longer sense the proper cues. The same is true when people must use new equipment. I still remember vividly the introduction of smokeless welders in a shop I was studying. The men who used that equipment became very suspicious when they could no longer see the smoke. They thought they were being poisoned by invisible smoke and that the new equipment was part of a plot perpetrated by the consultant to take advantage of their ignorance. No one had thought it important to anticipate their anxiety. After all, the new machines were easier and better to work with than the old, weren't they? And shouldn't people feel good about having better equipment?

Loss of Capacity to Affect Oneself or One's World

The loss of the capacity to affect oneself or one's world is probably the single most threatening experience of the contemporary industrial world. It is this feeling of being perennially victimized which has led to a wide range of reactions—race riots, consumerism, hostility to even well-conceived governmental action, and similar behavior. This feeling was given added impetus in managerial circles by the displacement of many middle management and professional people during the recession in the early 1970s. People who thought they had stable positions in their organizations and in their communities suddenly discovered that they had neither. I have frequently seen the same phenomenon in manufacturing organizations following ill-conceived, mechanistic change processes that then took years to unscramble. This phenomenon is magnified in organizations that rotate managers. People in these organizations inevitably feel that they cannot readily be heard because the manager isn't around long enough to understand them. They therefore organize themselves in such a way that it is impossible for the manager to penetrate their organizational armor. Visiting such plants or offices is like being in enemy territory. Managers experience this same loss of capacity to act when they themselves lose some control of their operations to more centralized processes or to higher level managements or to technical specialists or when they are threatened with being displaced, through, for example, work enrichment programs.

Aging and the Experience of Loss

The most common experience of loss is that which comes with aging. This is especially vivid for people in managerial ranks who frequently find old knowledge obsolete and experiences devalued; they suffer a diminution of competitive spirit while they are simultaneously threatened with younger competitors and new demands from the marketplace. The requirement that managers become more professional carries with it the implication that they are no longer good enough, no matter how hard they have worked nor how adequately they may have performed up to that point. The loss of youth is the most painful loss experience, for it threatens the capacity for adaptation and mastery and increases the threat of being dependent on other people.

As is evident from these illustrations, the experience of loss is costly to the organization as well as to individuals. Whatever the personal reactions may be, one way or another they become manifest in decreased organizational effectiveness and, simultaneously, in increased difficulty in effecting adaptive change. Therefore it becomes important to consider how to cope with these phenomena, which I will now do in depth.

COPING MECHANISMS

With this as background, let us return to the three questions with which we began. We have already responded to the first: Why is the experience of loss so significant and how does it have its effect? The answer to the second (What implications does the significance of this experience have for the manager and his family?) and the third (What implications does it have for organizational practices, particularly those relating to people?) lies in the fact that the experience of loss drains the energies of people as they fight depression and causes them to lose their positive motivation. This loss experience also results in physical symptoms and in psychological withdrawal from the environment of which they are a part.

What can the manager do to alert himself to the loss experience and to set in motion processes to counteract loss?

It is likely that the manager, concerned with his own family, will observe the loss experiences there first. The chances are that he will already have moved more than once in his career and will have observed the effects of moving on his spouse and children, as well as on himself. He will have sensed their feelings of regret for what they left behind and the time required for adaptation in the new setting. Some of his children may already have grown and moved on to form families of their own, another type of loss for him and his wife. Probably he will also have observed certain losses in himself and for himself, both physiological and psychological, as a result of losing those, with whom he had worked over a period of years, who themselves have moved on. Even in promotion he will have left behind many persons, places, and activities that he enjoyed and regretted leaving.

In his managerial role he will have responsibility for the movement of people both hierarchically and physically, for reasons of organization and reorganization, for reformulating work processes, and so on. Each move will pose problems for him which will not go away by themselves. Thus the implication is that for the most effective use of family and organizational resources he must attune himself to the loss experience so that he can be alert to it, anticipate it, repair it, and facilitate the restitution process.

In addition, organizations have long recognized the more overt physical needs of people. They have been concerned about the layout of machines and equipment, of offices and grounds. They have been alert to the implications of physical safety and environmental hazards and of the need for adequate lighting and other features of the work environment and their relationship to work effectiveness. But they have been less alert to psychological needs in any sophisticated way. However, as two generations of research have already indicated, if managements expect people to be work-motivated, to have loyalty and concern for the organization and its work, managements must give even more careful attention to the psychological needs of people—that is, to psychological man—or they will be forever doomed to manipulating carrots-and-sticks in a futile effort to sustain motivation and foster identification with the organization.

How can the manager cope with the loss experience? Before outlining steps which may be helpful, it is important for the manager to keep in mind that whatever efforts he undertakes, they have the advantage of the momentum of the already operating compensatory process of restitution. That is, just as a spider immediately goes at repairing its web, so people try to repair their social webs. The almost reflexive impulse to begin repairing his psychological injury provides the individual with a ready psychological handle for coping with loss and provides the organization with leverage to maximize its loss-countering efforts.

I propose five steps, the first two having to do with the manager's efforts and the remaining three with broader organizational activities.

Need for Awareness

The first important step, whether for family or business situations, is for managers to become *aware* of the loss experience in themselves and in others. This statement may seem trite; but, unless a person can become attuned to the loss experience he will not have the sensitivity to deal with it when it occurs.

One way to increase awareness is for a person to think about the various kinds of losses he has experienced and what kinds of feelings he has had in connection with them. Next, he can observe his own behavior to see how he responds to even small losses. From his own observations of himself, and others, he might begin to experience the depth and power of the feelings of loss.

For example, after a group of managers have worked together intensely on an organizational problem and then returned to greater concentration on their usual activities, they will likely feel some sadness at separating from each other, despite their eagerness to return to their normal duties. This sadness may reflect itself in the heavy emotional quality of the last day, in the jokes of the previous day which deny the sadness, and even in the early departure of some (for presumably other reasons) because they can't take good-byes.

Managers can review the feelings they had when they had to leave one location for another, one position for another, or one boss for another. Despite whatever positive feelings there were in each change, no doubt they will recall the underlying regret.

In organizations, depression is often obvious. Usually it is accompanied by the feeling that the problems to be dealt with are impossible to solve or that no one in power really cares or that those in the organization are incapable. Sometimes increase in trivial complaints, medical office visits, and even accidents are reflections of these feelings. A manager should pay close attention to words and behavior which indicate self-deprecation.

In the family one can observe how relatives cope with the loss experience. Everyone has frequent opportunity to observe subtle reactions as people lose friends, skills, confidence, support, and so on.

Furthermore, the stress that follows loss usually becomes more intense because the person must also cope with the demands of the new situation. The experience of loss, on the one hand, and the pressure of new demands, on the other, is or becomes the core stress of change. Both pressures are reflected in increased restlessness, depressed moods, irritability, physical symptoms, withdrawal from others, the appearance of sadness, and a greater sense of fatigue. Those pressures are often also reflected in a more intense busyness or in an artificial cheerfulness.

The manager must be aware of the fact that people will experience the pain of loss without necessarily giving any outward signs that they are doing so. Often this is because they think they should not express such feelings because they are supposed to maintain a "stiff upper lip" or because they can't accept pity and compassion or simply because they have steeled themselves against recognizing any such feelings. For some people, the simplest way of dealing with such threats is to pretend they don't exist. The implication of this is that they will tend to hide their feelings about many loss experiences even from themselves. Just as a small child will pull a blanket over his head to cope with the imagined threat in the darkness, so the adult calls into play the primitive defense of denial. The consequence of this is that the ordinary person denies many feelings of loss and, particularly, feelings of depression associated with loss and, therefore, is little aware of how this phenomenon affects him and his work. A corollary in the managerial situation occurs when managers are relatively insensitive to the significance of this phenomenon and fail to take it into account when changing a subordinate's circumstances or when they simply assume that the employee will compensate for whatever damage has occurred. The reader of this chapter, for example, may assert that the loss problem doesn't exist; and, even if it did, it has no significance for him or his organization.

Talk About Loss

Once a person becomes sufficiently aware of feelings of loss to know when they are arising or are likely to arise, the most immediately fruitful prophylactic is to talk about them. People can sometimes bear seemingly impossible emotional burdens when they are able to talk about them. When feelings are put into words, they can be dissipated or acted on with conscious intent. If they cannot be verbalized, they must be held in, often compelling people to act on the basis of impulses of which they are not aware and allowing no release from the anguish.

A person who has had a loss experience, or anticipates one, would do well to talk to someone else about it. When a person dies, those who mourn him frequently talk about him and in the talking gradually dissipate their feelings. This is the purpose of having friends pay condolence calls. The same process, though less dramatic, is helpful in all loss experiences. Thus if one loses a job, or has to give up the location he likes or associates he prefers, or a department he has built, he should find a way of talking to someone else about it.

In the Organization. Any manager, to whom others report, should create opportunities in his routine discussions with his subordinates for them to talk about their experiences of loss. When a man has accepted a transfer or a prospective move, for example, the boss might well say, "I know you're going to miss those people" or he may even ask, "Who are you going to miss most when you leave that job?" Such questions legitimize the opportunity for the subordinate to recall and recount the prospect of losses. Then the manager might ask, "How are you going to replace in your new assignment those things or people that you value so highly and that you will certainly miss?" This makes it possible for the subordinate to begin thinking out loud about not only what he will miss but also the importance of doing something to foster the restitution process. The same questions might be asked about what his family will miss, if they are making a physical move to another community, and how the reconstitution process can be set in motion for them. The manager might even inquire how he or the organization can be helpful to the person or to the family in restoring the supports they need, thus legitimizing the right and responsibility of the subordinate to call upon him and the organization for appropriate help in the adaptation process. After all, if the organization has created the psychological problem for the individual or his family or both, it certainly has the responsibility to help him cope with it.

Where groups of people are involved, this same thing might be done in the form of group discussions about changes so that the individuals involved can together share their feelings, publicly legitimize their right to have them, recognize their validity, and not be embarrassed for allowing their feelings to rise to the surface. Only by having people do so can the negative effects of loss begin to be counteracted. In effect, such expressions constitute a psychological wake, a group mourning process.

(Incidentally, I think it should be mandatory in all management training programs to teach managers to recognize and deal with such problems.)

Ideally prospective changes should be discussed this way in advance so that the feelings of loss do not interfere with effective adaptation to the changes. Too often managers try to reassure people that the changes will not hurt them or that everything will be all right. Such reassurances have little effect. In mergers they have become the signal that painful changes are indeed coming.

Some people would argue that in a competitive enterprise there is no room for dealing with feelings and certainly no room for dealing with them in this way. In addition, they would say that managers are incompetent to use even these simple psychological techniques. I contend that if the competitiveness within a business is of such a degree that it destroys that business's own most important resources (people), or even makes them less effective, then that business is deceiving itself and will pay an inordinate price for what it is doing. Furthermore, these simple ways of hearing people's painful problems, making it possible for them to talk about the problems, and evolving ways of coping with them do not require advanced, sophisticated, psychological thinking, and they are methods well within the capacity of practically all managers.

In the Family. The same principle applies in the family. If the family is able to look together at what is happening to them, to talk about it, to anticipate it, and to mourn their loss, they are likely to be more cohesive and to adapt better to their new circumstances. If certain kinds of losses can be anticipated, as in terminal illness or a move from one place to another, it is wise to talk about them long in advance so that the detachment process can begin early and occur slowly, allowing the people to ready themselves step-by-step. By doing so, they also begin to mourn the losses. The more acute and unexpected the loss, the greater the emotional shock that follows, and the more difficult it is to cope with.

For example, when one is going to be moving his family, the family might do well also to read a book like Edith Ruina's *Moving*.[3] That leads to practical planning and the discussion of feelings. The opportunity for the children to talk about their anger at leaving old friends and resources provides a way for them to discharge this anger, if the parents are not afraid of the expression of anger.

This principle is best illustrated by what happened in a hospital in which many of the staff had worked for a period of years. The building of a new hospital was planned. After the architects had talked with the staff, the architectural plans were posted on the bulletin boards of the old hospital. The staff talked about the plans and the renderings. They studied particularly their own areas. When the basic framework of the new building was up, there was an open house for visitors, and the staff showed the visitors around, pointing out, among other features, what were to be their own private spaces. The staff participated in the further planning for the new hospital. When the hospital was finally completed, they helped move their own belongings. Then they served as guides for another open house. Gradually they gave up the old while accepting the new; both processes went on simultaneously. In a contrasting situation, moving from a decrepit hospital to an excellent new one but without such a process, the staff could find nothing right about the new hospital for many months.

Mourning, as Dr. Alfred A. Messer of the Georgia Mental Health Institute points out, is a distinct process that involves dealing with one's emotional reactions and attitudes toward loss.[4] One has to go through the experiences of disbelief and protest, of overidentification with what had gone before, of being self-centered in trying to cope with the loss, and of feeling abandoned. The work of mourning involves the dissolution of the old ties and the mortification of them together with the establishment of new ones. When self-esteem has been battered by the loss, love and attention must be supplied so that the person begins to feel worthy again and finds support in his effort to recover.

---

[3] Edith Ruina, *Moving: A Common-Sense Guide to Relocating Your Family* (New York: Funk & Wagnalls, 1970).

[4] Alfred A. Messer, "Mourning the Death of a President," *Boston Sunday Globe* (November 22, 1970).

Company Action Plan

The third step in coping with loss is for the organization to evolve a plan of action for confrontation, adaptation, and restitution. This can be done in a number of ways. Preretirement programs are one way. Steps in the right direction would be asking prospective retirees, beginning at age sixty, what their retirement plans are going to be, setting up a retirement counseling program and preretirement discussions, and clarifying what resources and services will be available on retirement.

The same principles can be extended to planning for an employee's family to relocate. Companies can do much to help their employees relocate by preparing the way in advance with information about new communities and by having local people available to help them get settled when they arrive. In one situation where six management people were moved, the company sent the wives to the new community to examine housing, schools, medical facilities, and other resources. The wives brought back snapshots of homes, schools, parks, and so on, to be discussed with their families. By the time the move occurred, there were already familiar images of what was to come and mutually supportive group solidarity among the wives.

It should be routine in all organizations for those who are to be promoted or reassigned to weigh the psychological cost of the change to themselves and to their families. Many organizations move people around routinely. Most of the time this is done under the guise of broadening the person. Yet, frequently, I find that such moves are for movement's sake and contribute little to the broadening process.

Few organizations make it a policy to convey to their managers the importance of group and family decisions to support prospective changes. Most firms take it for granted that the manager wants a promotion and therefore offer it, assuming that from there on there will be no problems. Managers, for their part, most often feel that if they don't accept the promotion or move, they will lose visibility. This in turn fosters the concept of the mobile manager who lives by temporary expedient arrangements to ensure fast promotion. Such a life style then makes the whole process of relationship to an organization a self-centered, exploitative one because consciously or unconsciously the manager pictures himself as being exploited on behalf of the organization. This labels many organizations as merely large-scale, manipulative, and game-playing firms that cannot render adequate service, produce dependable products, stand behind trustworthy guarantees, evolve integrated performance, or foster those other qualities that give a business character. It is not without reason that all of these problems are in the forefront of contemporary consumer concern and contribute significantly to managerial frustration.

Dr. Jean S. Felton, director of the Los Angeles County Occupational Health Services, has evolved a counseling program in cooperation with the Department of Psychiatry of the University of Southern California, School of Medicine. This counseling program serves employees who have recently experienced the loss of an immediate member of the family. Employees use the service on self-referral or when the health service identifies those who are in mourning by reviewing the employees' bereavement leaves. The counseling service is carried on primarily by nurses and psychologists and is based on studies that show that both illness and death rates are higher in surviving spouses than in others of the same age and sex.[5]

According to a study by Dr. David Rosenthal of the National Institute of Mental Health, 90,000 Americans were hospitalized in 1967 for depression and "many times more never found their way to a hospital." [6] This is merely one indication of the pervasiveness of the phenomenon.

In short, wherever there are likely to be continuing and repetitive loss experiences, managements would do well to set up institutional modes for dealing with them.

Relating to the Community. The same principle regarding the experience of loss extends to the organization's relationship to the community of which it is a part. Often a plant must be closed. Sometimes it is the economic mainstay of the host community. The closing leaves the whole community with a loss experience. The confrontation-adaptation-restitution process in such a circumstance is illustrated by what happened when the American Oil Company closed its refinery in Neodesha, Kansas. Its planning began well in advance.

[5] Jean S. Felton, "Occupational Health: Government Program for County Employees," *Journal of the American Medical Association*, Vol. 217 (July 5, 1971), pp. 56–60.

[6] Dr. David Rosenthal, *Boston Globe* (April 24, 1972).

A year prior to the closing, a full-time coordinator was appointed to manage it. After a public announcement was made, discussions with employees, union leadership, community officials, and news media representatives followed. The company implemented a plan to find employees new jobs, keep them appraised of their benefits and opportunities, find new industry for the community, and turn over its property to the community for an industrial park. By the time the plant was closed, only 28 of 200 employees had not yet been placed. The company engaged a private employment agency to help them, and eventually all former refinery workers who wanted jobs were employed elsewhere. As a result of the new industry that was attracted to the industrial park, the 200 lost jobs were replaced by 300 new ones.

Another example is Owens-Illinois' transformation of its Bahama forestry operation into a sugar plantation. The company saw to it that the local economy would not be destroyed while new trees were maturing.

Maintain the Organizational Ideal

A fourth step in coping with a loss experience is to deal with the loss of the organizational ideal. Businesses these days are so preoccupied with goals they forget that goals are subsidiary to purposes. When there are no purposes, people can't be "for" anything. They feel themselves to be exploited in the interest of attaining another dollar for the stockholders or the boss. It is this feeling of exploitation for little long-run purpose that has alienated many people from business and has led to much of the contemporary criticism of business. Executives increasingly will have to be concerned with purpose if people, in turn, are to have long-term concern for their organizations. This means that top management groups will have to sit down together more frequently to ask what they are in business for and what they would like to leave behind when their time with their organizations is over. Such a formulation of purpose in keeping with the ego ideals of the individual executives gives rise to a collective effort. Goals represent steps in the attainment of whatever that ideal is. Subsequently such a set of purposes becomes the charter for the organization and by continuous discussion is open to continuing modification by those who give substantial portions of their lives to the organization.

Only a sense of purpose makes a sacrifice worthwhile; only a sense of having done something for the common good makes it possible for one to believe he has used his life well. For some top management groups such discussions may seem maudlin and inappropriate. Others may prefer exhortation, persuasion, flag-waving, and similar temporary expedient devices. I find in the organizations with which I work that such a mutual understanding of common purpose enhances the sense of being in it together and makes clearer the need for one another to attain that common purpose. This is in contrast to the usual method of playing people off against each other to their mutual destruction and to that of the organization. Top management groups should have an annual retreat where such things can be talked about, instead of the usual routine facts and figures, and instead of exhortative and sometimes utterly useless meetings at which, usually well lubricated by alcohol, colleagues arrive at temporary liaisons to assure themselves of each other's friendship for survival purposes. Once a sense of purpose has been established, arrived at out of people's wishes and commitments, this provides the most important psychological device for keeping people together and developing organizational momentum in a clearly defined direction.

Such an effort on an annual basis is a preventive device. It becomes particularly important when drastic organizational changes have had to take place, when diverse groups of people have had to be brought together, when merger has occurred, or when there has been a significant shift in leadership. If such group meetings do not take place, then there is an increase in internal resistance and an inhibition of the capacity to act cohesively and forcefully. Deadwood increases as motivation dies; depression follows the experience of loss, rejection, and desertion.

Managerial awareness of and concern for the loss problem is not merely a "do-gooder" interest. It is also an important matter of self-interest. All organizations increasingly will have to evaluate the human cost of loss and change. Organizations are already called upon to think of the cost of their effects on the environment. The next step in the process of social evolution will be to weigh the costs of organizational influences on people. We already know the cost of disruption in alienation, increase in psychosomatic illness, decrease in productivity, and the chronic depression that many people experience when the manner in which they are managed maximizes their loss experience and disrupts their sources of gratification and support. In some countries, such abrupt hiring and firing, reassignment, demotion, and so on, are unacceptable because of their destructive effects on people. These will become increasingly unacceptable in the United States. It is predictable that, ultimately, psychological pollution, precipitated by arbitrary and unthinking leadership action, will become unacceptable and subject to compensation just as environmental pollution and contamination and its effects are now subject to compensation. Managers, therefore, must be thinking about the impact of their decisions for the experience of loss on people and the possible costs and consequences for both individuals and organizations.

Job Changes

The fifth step in coping with the loss experience is for the organization and the individual to think specifically about the import of job changes. This is particularly true with managerial and executive jobs.

In thinking about the promotion and reassignment of employees, organizational representatives should look more closely at the characteristics of behavior which the prospective job requires and also at the degree to which those characteristics are the ingrained characteristics of the individual. I refer here specifically to preferred behavioral characteristics. Organizations move too many managers into too many jobs on the assumption that those managers will be able to change their behavior in keeping with whatever the behavioral requirements of the job may be. People cannot change their behavior that readily; in fact, there are severe limitations to how much people are able to change. A characteristically active man will find himself at a loss in a situation where more often he must remain passive. By the same token, less competitive people will find themselves to have lost their favorite ways of behaving when they are required to be more competitive. A move into a new position may cause a man not only to lose his familiar ways of getting a job done, but also to become separated from key people who supported him.

For example, it is an old cliché in management that when a good salesman is promoted to sales manager, the organization loses a good salesman and acquires a poor sales manager. The preferred ways of behaving for a good salesman often have to do with meeting people, pleasing them, persuading them, and serving them. In short, a good salesman needs to please and be liked by people. He needs continuous contact with people. A sales manager, by way of contrast, needs, particularly, to support his salesmen against the repetitive rebuffs of the selling experience. He is deprived of direct contact with the customer. When a good salesman is placed in a sales manager's position, he has to behave in ways different from those which he prefers and is used to. He therefore experiences loss and new demands; he cannot act in a way that makes a sales manager effective. The same thing happens with respect to most other managerial jobs. Therefore, careful thinking is required on the part of the organization about the matching of characteristic individual behavior and situational requirements for behavior.

In addition to thinking about the match between man and job, individual managers should be encouraged to weigh carefully their own behavioral characteristics. In training programs and in discussions with their superiors, personnel executives, and similar organization agents, managers should be encouraged and even required to spell out in detail self-descriptions that include their preferred ways of handling aggression, affection, and dependency and to try to define their own ego ideals. They should then be invited to compare these self-descriptions (verified and corroborated by their discussions with their superiors in regular appraisal interviews) with the behavior requirements of the new job they are being asked to consider. Often managers are so hungry for promotion that they will be just as unthinking as their superiors about their chances for succeeding in their new jobs. The resulting negligence often leads to disappointment on both sides. When a manager understands that such self-evaluation and organizational evaluation is for the purpose of maximizing his potential success and minimizing the downside risk, and that he will not be passed over for subsequent promotion if the prospective job is not something for which he is suited, then more managers will more comfortably make more reasonable choices to the mutual advantage of the individual and the organization.

CONCLUSION

Everyone carries with him, in varying degrees, the psychological burdens of loss from a lifetime of experience. As a corollary, everyone is vulnerable, in varying degrees, to the threat of additional loss. The theme of our age is change. All change necessarily involves the experience of loss and therefore produces psychological symptoms of consequence to the individual and to the organization. By and large, managements are unaware of the significance of the loss experience as it relates to the organization. The consequence is that many actions are taken which maximize the loss experience and result in both individual symptoms and even more massive resistance to organizational change. Fortunately, the experience of loss sets in motion a restitutive process. Managers who are aware of the phenomenon of loss and the restitutive process can protect themselves, their families, their subordinates, and their organization from the undue consequences of loss with a minimum of psychological effort. Managements, aware of these phenomena, can readily set in motion processes that will help people avoid many of the negative consequences of loss experience and simultaneously foster a closer, more effective working relationship between people and organizations. In an era of increasingly rapid organizational change, when people feel more and more alienated and alone on the one hand and managements strive with increasing frustration to sustain identification with the organization, loyalty, and investment in task on the other, it becomes imperative to look ever more closely at how these two separate needs of the individual and the organization can be welded into a common purpose from which the individual, the organization, and the community all profit.

CHAPTER 6

Management by Whose Objectives?

PSYCHOLOGICAL MAN as adaptive and interacting, as unfolding and maturing, and in pursuit of mastering his own fate runs repeatedly afoul of those managerial processes and practices built on the great jackass fallacy. The poor fit of man with the managerial process is particularly evident in the more common management techniques. Among the most widespread, and therefore a good medium for illustration, is management by objectives. Turning from the life stage of the individual to the practice of a management technique is an abrupt shift from one dimension of the person to a single dimension of the organization. However, these abrupt shifts permit us to sample different aspects of the individual and the organization and, by so doing, test the consistency, validity, and usefulness of the psychological man theory.

Despite the fact that the concept of management by objectives (MBO) has by this time become an integral part of the managerial process, the typical MBO effort perpetuates and intensifies hostility, resentment, and distrust between a manager and his subordinates. As currently practiced, it is really just industrial engineering with a new name, based on jackass psychology, applied to higher managerial levels and with the same resistances.

Obviously, somewhere between the concept of MBO and its implementation, something has gone seriously wrong. Coupled with performance appraisal, the intent is to follow the Frederick Taylor[1]

---

[1] Frederick Taylor Winslow, "Principles of Scientific Management," in *Scientific Management* (New York: Harper & Row, 1947).

tradition of a more rational management process; that is, which people are to do what, who is to have effective control, and how is compensation to be related directly to individual achievement. The MBO process, essentially, is an effort to be fair and reasonable, to predict performance and judge it more carefully and, presumably, to provide individuals with an opportunity to be self-motivating by setting their own objectives.

The intent of clarifying job obligations and measuring performance against a man's own goals seems reasonable enough. The concern for having both superior and subordinate consider the same matters in reviewing the performance of the subordinate is eminently sensible. The effort to come to common agreement on what constitutes the subordinate's job is highly desirable.

Yet, like most rationalizations in the Taylor tradition, MBO as a process is one of the greatest of managerial illusions because it fails to take adequately into account the deeper emotional components of motivation.

In this chapter, I shall indicate how I think management by objectives, as currently practiced in most organizations, is self-defeating and serves simply to increase pressure on the individual. By doing so, I do not reject either MBO or performance appraisal. Rather, by raising the basic question "Whose objectives?" I propose to suggest how they might be made more constructive devices for effective management. The issues I shall raise have largely to do with psychological considerations and, particularly, with the assumptions about motivation which underlie these techniques.

THE "IDEAL" PROCESS[2]

Since management by objectives is closely related to performance appraisal and review, I shall consider these together as one practice that is intended

---

[2] In this part of the chapter, which defines the ideal process and the major problems inherent in it, I draw heavily on the work of these authors, in sequence: Alva F. Kindall and James Gatza, "Positive Program for Performance Appraisal," *Harvard Business Review* (November–December 1963), p. 153; Herbert H. Meyer, Emanuel Kay, and John R. P. French, Jr., "Split Roles in Performance Appraisal," *Harvard Business Review* (January–February 1965), p. 123; Ishwar Dayal, "Role Analysis Techniques in Job Description," *California Management Review*, XI:4 (1969), p. 47; Stanley Sloan

to measure and judge performance

to relate individual performance to organizational goals

to clarify both the job to be done and the expectations of accomplishment

to foster the increasing competence and growth of the subordinate

to enhance communications between superior and subordinate

to serve as a basis for judgments about salary and promotion

to stimulate the subordinate's motivation

to serve as a device for organizational control and integration

Major Problems

According to contemporary thinking, the ideal process should proceed in five steps: (1) individual discussion with his superior of the subordinate's description of his own job, (2) establishment of short-term performance targets, (3) meetings with the superior to discuss progress toward targets, (4) establishment of checkpoints to measure progress, and (5) discussion between superior and subordinate at the end of a defined period to assess the results of the subordinate's efforts. In *ideal* practice, this process occurs against a background of more frequent, even day to day, contacts and is separate from salary review. But, in *actual* practice, there are many problems. Consider:

No matter how detailed the job description, it is essentially static, that is, a series of statements. However, the more complex the task and the more flexible a man must be in it, the less any fixed statement of job elements will fit what he does. Thus the higher a man rises in an organization and the more varied and subtle his work, the more difficult it is to pin down objectives that represent more than a fraction of his effort.

---

and Alton C. Johnson, "Performance Appraisal . . . Where Are We Headed?" *The Personnel Administrator*, 14:5 (1969), p. 12; Philip R. Kelly, "Reappraisal of Appraisals," *Harvard Business Review* (May–June 1958), p. 59; Robert A. Howell, "A Fresh Look at Management by Objectives," *Business Horizons*, 10:3 (1967), p. 51; Albert W. Schrader, "Let's Abolish the Annual Performance Review," *Management of Personnel Quarterly* (Fall 1969), p. 20; George H. Labovitz, "In Defense of Subjective Executive Appraisal," *Academy of Management Journal*, 12:3 (1969), p. 293; Larry E. Greiner, D. Paul Leitch, and Louis B. Barnes, "Putting Judgment Back Into Decisions," *Harvard Business Review* (March–April 1970), p. 59; George Strauss and Leonard R. Sayles, *Personnel: The Human Problems of Management* (Englewood Cliffs, N. J.: Prentice-Hall, 1967), p. 564.

With preestablished goals and descriptions, little weight can be given to the areas of discretion open to the individual but not incorporated into his job description or objectives. I am referring here to those spontaneously creative activities an innovative executive might choose to do or to those tasks a responsible executive sees which need to be done. As we move more toward a service society, in which tasks are less well defined but spontaneity of service and self-assumed responsibility are crucial, this becomes pressing.

Most job descriptions are limited to what a man himself does in his work. They do not adequately take into account the increasing interdependence of managerial work in organizations. This limitation becomes more important as the impact of social and organizational factors on individual performance becomes better understood. The more a man's effectiveness depends on what other people do, the less he himself can be held responsible for the outcome of his efforts.

If a primary concern in performance review is counseling the subordinate, appraisal should consider and take into account the total situation in which the superior and subordinate are operating. In addition, this should take into account the relationship of the subordinate's job to other jobs rather than to his alone. In counseling, much of the focus is in helping the subordinate learn to negotiate the system. To my knowledge, there is no provision in most reviews and no place on appraisal forms to report and record such discussion.

The setting and evolution of objectives are made over too brief a period of time to provide for adequate interaction among different levels of an organization. This militates against opportunity for peers, both in the same work unit and in complementary units, to work together to develop objectives for maximum integration. Thus, both the setting of objectives and the appraisal of performance make little contribution toward the development of teamwork and more effective organizational self-control.

Coupled with these problems is the difficulty superiors experience when they undertake appraisals. Douglas McGregor complained that the major reason appraisal failed was that superiors disliked playing God by making judgments about another man's worth.[3] He likened

---

[3] Douglas McGregor, "An Uneasy Look at Performance Appraisal," *Harvard Business Review* (May–June 1957), p. 89.

the superior's experience to the inspection of assembly line products and contended that his revulsion was against being inhuman. To cope with this problem, McGregor recommended that an individual should set his own goals, check them out with his superior, and use the appraisal session as a counseling device. Thus, the superior would act as an adviser to help the subordinate achieve his own goals instead of serving as a dehumanized inspector of products.

Parenthetically, I doubt very much that the failure of appraisal stems from playing God or feeling inhuman. My own observation leads me to believe that managers define their appraisal of others as a hostile, aggressive act that they unconsciously feel is hurting or destroying the other person. The appraisal situation, therefore, gives rise to powerful, paralyzing feelings of guilt that make it extremely difficult for most executives to be constructively critical of subordinates.

Objectivity Plea

Be that as it may, the more complex and difficult the appraisal process and the setting and evaluation of objectives, the more pressing the cry for objectivity. This is a vain plea. Every organization is a social system, a network of interpersonal relationships. A man may do an excellent job by objective standards of measurement, but he may fail miserably as a partner, subordinate, superior, or colleague. It is a commonplace that more people fail to be promoted for personal reasons than for technical inadequacy.

Furthermore, since every subordinate is a component of his superior's efforts to achieve his own goals, he will inevitably be appraised on how well he works with his superior and helps the latter meet his own needs. A considerable subjective element necessarily enters into every appraisal and goal-setting experience.

The plea for objectivity is vain for another reason. The greater the emphasis on measurement and quantification, the more likely the subtle, nonmeasurable elements of the task will be sacrificed. Quality of performance, therefore, frequently loses out to quantification.

A Case Example. A manufacturing plant that produces high-quality, high-prestige products and is backed by a reputation for customer consideration and service has instituted an MBO program. It is well-worked-out and has done much to clarify both individual goals and organizational performance. It is an important component of the company's professional management style that has led to the firm's commendable growth.

But an interesting, and ultimately destructive, process has been set in motion. The managers are beginning to worry because when they now ask why something has not been done, they hear from each other, "That isn't in my goals." They complain that customer service is deteriorating. The vague goal, "improve customer service," is almost impossible to measure. There is therefore heavy concentration on those subgoals that can be measured. Thus, time per customer, number of customer calls, and similar measures are used as guides in judging performance. The *less* time per customer and the *fewer* the calls, the better the customer service manager meets his objectives. He is cutting costs, increasing profit—and killing the business. Worse still, he hates himself.

Most of the managers in that organization joined it because of its reputation for high quality and good service. They want to make good products and earn the continued admiration of their customers, as well as the envy of their industry. When they are not operating at that high level, they feel guilty. They become angry with themselves and the company. They feel that they might just as well be working for someone else who admittedly does a sloppy job of quality control and could hardly care less about service.

The same problem exists with respect to the development of personnel, which is another vague goal that is hard to measure in comparison with subgoals that are measurable. If asked, each manager can name a younger man as his potential successor, particularly if his promotion depends on doing so; but no one has the time, or indeed feels that he is being paid, to train the younger man thoroughly. By the same token, there is no way in that organization to measure how well a manager does in developing another.

THE MISSED POINT

All of the problems with objectives and appraisals outlined in the example discussed in the foregoing section indicate that MBO does not work well despite what some companies think about their programs. The underlying reason is that MBO misses the whole human point.

To see how the point is being missed, let us follow the typical MBO process. Characteristically, top management sets its corporate goal for the coming year. This may be in terms of return on investment, sales, production, growth, or other measurable factors.

Within this frame of reference, reporting managers may then be asked how much their units intend to contribute toward meeting that goal or they may be asked to set their own goals relatively independent of the corporate goal. If they are left free to set their own goals, these in any case are expected to be higher than those they had the previous year. Usually, each reporting manager's range of choices is limited to his option for a piece of the organizational action or to improvement of specific statistics. In some cases, it may also include obtaining specific training or skills.

Once a reporting manager decides on his unit's goals and has them approved by his superior, those become the manager's goals. Presumably, he has committed himself to what he wants to do. He has said it and he is responsible for it. He is thereafter subject to being hoisted with his own petard.

Now, let us reexamine this process closely: the whole method is based on a short-term, ego-centrically oriented perspective and an underlying reward-punishment psychology. The typical MBO process puts the reporting manager in much the same position as a rat in a maze who has choices between only two alternatives. The experimenter who puts the rat in the maze assumes that the rat wants the food reward; if he cannot presume that, he starves the rat to make sure he wants the food.

Management by objectives differs only in that it permits the man himself to choose his own bait from a limited range of choices. Having done so, the MBO process assumes that he will (1) work hard to get it, (2) be pushed internally by reason of his commitment, and (3) make himself responsible to his organization for doing so.

In fairness to most managers, they certainly try, but not without increasing resentment and complaint for feeling like rats in a maze, guilt for not paying attention to those parts of the job not in their objectives, and passive resistance to the mounting pressure for ever higher goals.

Personal Goals

The MBO process leaves out the answers to such questions as: What are the manager's personal objectives? What does he need and want out of his work? How do his needs and wants change from year to year? What relevance do organizational objectives and his part in them have to such needs and wants?

Obviously, no objectives will have significant incentive power if they are forced choices unrelated to a man's underlying dreams, wishes, and personal aspirations. For example, if a salesman relishes the pleasure of his relationships with his hard-earned but low-volume customers, this is a powerful need for him. Suppose his boss, who is concerned about increasing the volume of sales, urges him to concentrate on the larger quantity customers, who will provide the necessary increase in volume, and then asks him how much of an increase he can achieve.

To work with the larger quantity customers means that the salesman will be less likely to sell to the individuals with whom he has well-established relationships and will be more likely to deal with purchasing agents, technical people, and staff specialists who will demand of him knowledge and information he may not have in sophisticated detail. Moreover, as a single salesman, his organization may fail to support him with technical help to meet these demands.

When this happens, he may not only lose his favorite way of operating, which had well served his own needs, but he may have demands put on him which cause him to feel inadequate. If he is being compelled to make a choice about the percent of sales volume increase he expects to attain, he may well do that but now under great psychological pressure. No one has recognized the psychological realities the salesman may have to face, let alone helped him to work with them. It is simply assumed that since his sales goal is a rational one, he will see its rationality and pursue it.

The problem may be further compounded if, as is not unusual, formal changes are made in the organizational structure: sales territories may be shifted, modes of compensation may be changed, problems of delivery may occur, and so on. All of these are factors beyond the salesman's control. Nevertheless, even with certain allowances, he is still held responsible for meeting his sales goal.

Psychological Needs

Lest the reader think the example just given is exaggerated or irrelevant, I know of a young sales manager who resigned his job, despite his success in it, because he chose not to be expendable in an organization that he felt regarded him only as an instrument for reaching a goal. Many young men are refusing to enter large organizations for just this reason.

Some readers may argue that my criticism is unfair, that many organizations start their planning and setting of objectives from below. Therefore, the company cannot be accused of putting the man in a maze; but it does so, just the same. In almost all cases, the only legitimate objectives to be set are those having to do with measurable increases in performance. This highlights, again, the question, "Whose objectives?" This question becomes more pressing in situations in which lower level people set their objectives, only to have them questioned by higher level managers and told their targets are not high enough.

Here you may well ask, "What's the matter with that? Aren't we in business, and isn't the purpose of the man's work to serve the requirements of the business?" The answer to both questions is, "Obviously." But that is only part of the story.

If a man's most powerful driving force is comprised of his needs, wishes, and personal aspirations combined with the compelling wish to look good in his own eyes for meeting those deeply held personal goals, then management by objectives should begin with *his* objectives. What does he want to do with his life? Where does he want to go? What will make him feel good about himself? What does he want to be able to look back on when he has expended his unrecoverable years?

At this point, some may say that these goals are his business. The company has other business, and it must assume that the man is interested in working in the company's business rather than in his own. That kind of differentiation is impossible. Everyone is always working toward meeting his psychological needs. Anyone who thinks otherwise and who believes such powerful internal forces can be successfully disregarded, or bought off for long, is deluding himself.

THE MUTUAL TASK

The organizational task becomes one of first understanding the man's needs and then, after assessing with him how well they can be met in this organization, doing what the organization needs to have done. Thus, the highest point of self-motivation arises when there is a complementary conjunction of the man's needs and the organization's requirements. The requirements of both mesh, interrelate, and become synergistic. The energies of man and organization are pooled for mutual advantage.

If the two sets of needs do not mesh, then a man has to fight himself and his organization in addition to doing the work that must be done and meeting the targets that have been set. In such a case, this requires that the subordinate and his boss evaluate together where the subordinate wants to go, where the organization is going, and how significant the discrepancy is. The man might well be better off somewhere else, and the organization might do better to have in his place someone else whose needs mesh better with the organization requirements.

Long-Run Costs

The issue of meshed interests is particularly relevant for middle-aged, senior-level managers. As indicated in Chapter 4, when men come into middle age, their values often begin to change, and they feel anew the pressure to accomplish many long-deferred dreams. When such wishes begin to stir, they begin to experience severe conflict.

Up to this point, they have committed themselves to the organization and have done sufficiently well in it to attain high rank. Usually, they are slated for even higher levels of responsibility. The organization has been good to them, and their superiors are depending on them to provide leadership to the company. They have been models for the younger men, whom they have urged to aspire to organizational heights. To think of leaving is to desert both their superiors and their subordinates.

Since there are few opportunities within the organization to talk about such conflict, they try to suppress their wishes. The internal pressure continues to mount until they finally make an impulsive break, surprising and dismaying both themselves and their colleagues. I can think of three vice presidents who have done just that.

The issue is, not so much that a manager decides to leave, but the cost of the manner of his departure. An early discussion with his superior about his personal goals would have enabled both to examine possible relocation alternatives within the organization. If there were none, then both the manager and his superior might have come to a better, more comfortable decision about separation. The organization would have had more time to make satisfactory alternative plans as well as to have taken steps to compensate for the manager's lagging enthusiasm. Lower level managers would then have seen the company as humane in its enlightened self-interest and would not have had to create fearful fantasies about what the top management conflicts were that had caused a good man to leave.

To place consideration of the managers' personal objectives first does not minimize the importance of the organization's goals. It does not mean there is anything wrong with the organization's need to increase its return on investment, its size, its productivity, or its other goals. However, I contend that it is ridiculous to make assumptions about the motivations of individuals and then to set up the means of increasing the pressures on people based on these often questionable assumptions. While there may be certain demonstrable short-run statistical gains, what are the long-run costs?

One cost is that people may leave; another, that they may fall back from competitive positions to plateaus. Why should an individual be expendable for someone else and sacrifice himself for something that is not part of his own cherished dreams? Still another cost may be the loss of the essence of the business: witness the case example of the manufacturing plant with the problem of deteriorating customer service. In that example, there had initially been no dialogue. Nobody heard what the managers said, what they wanted, where they wanted to go, where they wanted the organization to go, and how they felt about the supposedly rational procedures that had been initiated. The underlying psychological assumption that management unconsciously made was that the managers *had to be made* more efficient; ergo, management by objectives.

Top management typically assumes that it alone has the prerogative to (1) set the objectives, (2) provide the rewards and targets, and

(3) drive anyone who works for the organization. As long as this re-ward-punishment psychology exists in any organization, the MBO appraisal process is certain to fail.

Many organizations make this issue worse by promising their young employees that they will have challenges, since they assume these people will be challenged by management's objectives. Man-agements are having difficulty, even when they have high turnover rates, hearing these youngsters say they could hardly care less for management's unilaterally determined objectives. Managements then become angry, complaining that the young people do not want to work or that they want to become presidents overnight.

What the young people are asking is: What about me and my needs? Who will listen? How much will management help me meet my own requirements while also meeting its objectives?

The power of this force is reflected in the finding that the more the subordinate participates in the appraisal interview by presenting his own ideas and beliefs, the more likely he is to feel that (1) the supe-rior is helpful and constructive, (2) some current job problems are being cleared up, and (3) reasonable future goals are being set.[4]

THE SUGGESTED STEPS

Given the validity of all the MBO problems I have been discussing to this point, there are a number of possibilities for coping with them. Here, I suggest three beginning steps.

Motivational Assessment

Every management by objectives program and its accompanying performance appraisal system should be examined in terms of the ex-tent to which it (1) expresses the conviction that people are patsies to be driven, urged, and manipulated and (2) fosters a genuine partner-ship between men and organization, in which each has some in-fluence over the other, as contrasted with the rat-in-the-maze rela-tionship.

It is not easy for the nonpsychologist to approach such problems

---

[4] Ronald J. Burke and Douglas S. Wilcox, "Characteristics of Effective Employee Performance Reviews and Developmental Interviews," *Personal Psychology*, 22:3 (1969), p. 291.

by himself, but there are clues to the solutions. One clue is how decisions about compensation, particularly bonuses, are made.

(1) A sales manager asked my opinion about an incentive plan for highly motivated salesmen who were in a seller's market. I asked why he needed one, and he responded, "To give them an incentive." When I pointed out that they were already highly motivated and apparently needed no incentive, he changed his rationale and said that the company wanted to share its success to keep the men identified with it and to express its recognition of their contribution. I asked, "Why not let them establish the reward related to performance?" The question startled him; obviously, if they were going to decide, who needed him? A fundamental aspect of his role, as he saw it, was to drive them ever onward, whether they needed it or not.

(2) A middle-management bonus plan tied to performance proved to be highly unsatisfactory in a plastic fabricating company. Frustrated that its well-intentioned efforts were not working and determined to follow precepts of participative management, ranking executives involved many people and departments in formulating a new one: personnel, control, marketing executives, and others—in fact, everyone but the managers who were to receive the bonuses. Top management is now dismayed that the new plan is as unsatisfactory as the old and is bitter that participation failed to work.

Another clue is the focus of company meetings. Some are devoted to intensifying the competition between units. Others lean heavily to exhortation and inspiration. Contrast these orientations with meetings in which people are appraised of problems and plan to cope with them.

Group Action

Every objectives and appraisal program should include group goal setting, group definition of both individual and group tasks, group appraisal of its accomplishments, group appraisal of each individual member's contribution to the group effort (without basing compensation on that appraisal), and shared compensation based on the relative success with which group goals are achieved. Objectives should include long-term as well as short-term goals.

The rationale is simple. Every managerial job is an interdependent task. Managers have responsibilities to each other as well as to their superiors. The reason for having an organization is to achieve more together than each could alone. Why, then, emphasize and reward individual performance alone based on static job descriptions? That can only orient people to both incorrect and self-centered goals. Where people are in complementary relationships, whether they report to the same superior or not, both horizontal and vertical goal formulation should be formalized, with regular, frequent opportunity for review of problems and progress. They should help each other define and describe their respective jobs, enhancing control and integration at the point of action.

In my judgment, for example, a group of managers (sales, promotion, advertising) reporting to a vice president of marketing should formulate their collective goals and define ways of both helping each other and of assessing each others' effectiveness in the common task. The group assessment of each manager's work should be a means of providing each with constructive feedback, not for determining pay. However, in addition to his salary, each should receive, as part of whatever additional compensation is offered, a return based on the group effort.

The group's discussion within itself and with its superior should include examination of organizational and environmental obstacles to goal achievement and, particularly, of what organizational and leadership supports are required to attain objectives. One important reason for this is that often people think there are barriers where none would exist if they initiated action. ("You mean the president really wants us to get together and solve this problem?")

Another reason is that frequently when higher management sets goals, it is unaware of significant barriers to achievement, which can make managers cynical. For example, if there is no comprehensive orientation and support program to help new employees adapt, then pressure on lower level managers to employ disadvantaged minority group members and to reduce their turnover can only be experienced by those managers as hollow mockery.

Appraisal of Appraisers

All management by objectives and appraisal programs should include regular appraisals of the manager by his subordinates, and these should be reviewed by the manager's superior. Based on such appraisals, every manager should be specifically compensated for how well he develops people. The very phrase "reporting to" reflects the fact that although the manager has the responsibility, his superior also has responsibility for what the manager does and how he does it.

In fact, both common sense and research indicate that the single most significant outside influence on how well the manager does his job is his superior. If that is the case, then the key environmental factor in task accomplishment and managerial growth is the relationship between the manager and his superior.

Objectives, therefore, should include not only the individual manager's personal and occupational goals but also the corporate goals he and his superior share in common. They should together appraise their relationship vis-à-vis both the manager's individual goals and their joint objectives, review what they have done together, and discuss the implications for their next joint steps.

A manager rarely is in a position to judge his superior's overall performance, but he can appraise him on the basis of how well the superior has helped him to do his job, how well the supervisor is helping him to increase his proficiency and visibility, what problems the supervisor poses for him, and what kinds of support he himself can use. Such feedback serves several purposes. Most important, it offers the superior some guidance on his own managerial performance. In addition, and particularly when the manager is protected by higher level review of his appraisal, it provides the supervisor with direct feedback on his own behavior. This is much more constructive than behind-the-back complaints and vituperative terminal interviews, cases in which the superior has no opportunity either to defend himself or correct his behavior. Every professional counselor has dealt with recently fired executives who did not know why they had been discharged for being poor superiors when, according to their information, their subordinates thought so much of them. It is, therefore, to every manager's advantage to have appraisal by his subordinates.

I am advocating a three-way performance appraisal system that will make it possible not only for the leader to evaluate the follower but vice versa too, and for peers to evaluate their interwork group relationships and their effectiveness in doing their collective task. Such a system also requires a compensation system that complements this combined effort.

Many compensation systems have as appendages either bonuses or piecework incentives. Bonuses and profit sharing have a paternalistic quality about them. Frequently they have little relationship to what the employee does directly in his work. If the president of a company decides one year to buy an airplane, there may be no profit to share that year. Incentive plans are literally carrot-and-stick. They work as long as people need the money and can be manipulated into that kind of psychological trap.

A compensation system should be: (1) competitive for the particular skill or discipline (engineer, steamfitter, secretary); (2) based additionally on individual performance; (3) based further on group achievement, the outcome of the efforts of the work group, however that is defined; (4) and based in part on system effectiveness, by which I mean the results of the total organization or of that segment of the organization over which the people who are being compensated have some control. Rewarding or penalizing people for forces over which they have no control has little if any motivational merit. However, to be fully motivational and to be tied to purpose, goals, and reality, a compensation system should always be part of a system of participation and involvement in which people can correct the internal conflicts, mistakes, and inefficiencies of the system of which they are a part. If such avenues are not present, then their anger and guilt will multiply, particularly when the compensation system is vitiated by correctable errors on which they cannot act.

THE BASIC CONSIDERATION

When the four organizational conditions for compensation I have just outlined do in fact exist, then it is appropriate to think of starting management by objectives with a consideration of each man's personal objectives. If the underlying attitude in the organization toward him is that he is but an object, there is certainly no point in starting with the man; nor is there any point in trying to establish his confidence in his superiors when he is not protected from their rivalry with him or when they are playing him off against his peers. Anyone who expressed his fears and innermost wishes under these circumstances would be a damned fool.

For reasons I have already indicated, it should be entirely legitimate in every business for these concerns to be the basis for individual objectives-setting. This is because the fundamental managerial consideration necessarily must be focused on the question: "How do we meet both individual and organizational purposes?" If a major intention of management by objectives is to enlist the self-motivated commitment of the individual, then that commitment must derive from the individual's powerful wishes to support the organization's goals; otherwise, the commitment will be merely incidental to his personal wishes.

Having said that, the real difficulty begins. How can any superior know what a subordinate's personal goals and wishes are if the subordinate himself is—as most of us are—not clear about them? How ethical is it for a superior to pry into a man's personal life? How can he keep himself from forming a negative judgment about a man who, he knows, is losing interest in his work or is not altogether identified with the company? How can he keep that knowledge from interfering with judgments he might otherwise make and opportunities he might otherwise offer? How often are the personal goals, particularly in middle age, temporary fantasies that are better not discussed? Can a superior who is untrained in psychology handle such information constructively? Will he perhaps do more harm than good?

These are critically important questions. And although I have discussed some of this material before, especially in Chapter 3, it deserves to be repeated here because of its relevance to these critical issues. Nevertheless, my answers should be taken as no more than beginning steps.

Ego Concepts

Living is a process of constant adaptation. A man's personal goals, wishes, and aspirations are continuously evolving and being continuously modified by his experiences. That is one reason why it is so difficult for an individual to specify concrete personal objectives. Nevertheless, each of us has a built-in road map, in the form of his ego ideal. Much of a person's ego ideal is unconscious, which is another reason why it is not clear to him.

Subordinate's Self-examination. Although a man cannot usually spell out his ego ideal, he can talk about those experiences that have been highly gratifying, even exhilarating, to him. He can specify those rare peak experiences that made him feel very good about himself. When he has an opportunity to talk about what he has found especially gratifying and also what he thinks would be gratifying to him, he is touching on central elements of his ego ideal.

Given the opportunity to talk about such experiences and wishes on successive occasions, a man can begin to spell out for himself the central thrust of his life. Reviewing all of the occupational choices he has made and the reasons for making them, he can begin to see the common threads in those choices and therefore the momentum of his personality. As these become clearer to him, he is in a better position to weigh alternatives against the mainstream of his personality.

For example, a man who has successively chosen occupational alternatives in which he was individually competitive and whose most exhilarating experiences have come from defeating an opponent or single-handedly vanquishing a problem would be unlikely to find a staff position exhilarating, no matter what it paid or what it was called. His ideal for himself is that of a vanquishing, competitive man.

The important concept here is that it is not necessary for a man to spell out concrete goals at any one point; rather, it is helpful to him and his organization if he is able to examine and review aloud on a continuing basis his thoughts and feelings about himself in relation to his work. Such a process makes it legitimate for him to bring his own feelings to consciousness and talk about them in the business context as the basis for his relationship to the organization.

By listening, and helping him to spell out how and what he feels, the superior does not *do* anything to the man, and therefore by that self-appraisal process cannot hurt him. The information serves both the man and his superior as a criterion for examining the relationship of the man's feelings and his personal goals, however dimly perceived, to organizational goals. Even if some of his wishes and aspirations are fantasies impossible to gratify, if it is legitimate to talk about them without being laughed at, he can compare them with the realities of his life and make more reasonable choices.

Even in the safest organizational atmosphere, for reasons already mentioned, it will not be easy for managers to talk about their goals. The best-intentioned supervisor is likely to be something less than a highly skilled interviewer. These two facts suggest that any effort to ascertain a subordinate's personal goals would be futile; but I think not.

The important point is, not how specific a statement any man can make, but the nature of a superior-subordinate relationship that makes it safe to explore such feelings and that gives first consideration to the man. In such a context, both subordinate and superior may come closer to evolving a man-organization fit than they otherwise might.

If this is the case, then the managerial task becomes one of alliance with the ego ideals of those employees one supervises rather than fighting the individuals or manipulating them in the psychological prison that is the contemporary hierarchical environment. That requires having transcendent purpose for an organization—not just an organizational goal but a purpose that makes it worthwhile for people to expend years of their lives in the organization.

Motivation, as I am using the term, has certain specific requirements of action on the part of the leader, whether supervisor, manager, or executive. First it requires that the leader form a supervisory alliance with his followers in which they together are focusing on mastering the external realities and the internal problems the organization faces. Instead of fighting each other as in the hierarchical mode of organization, with its heavy emphasis on dependency, they are on the same side fighting the common enemy—reality. Their question to each other and the leader's question to them is, "What are we going to do about it?" Thus those with greater and lesser responsibilities are engaged in a common task with mutual support against an outside enemy, and the resources of the whole organization are mobilized to help them accomplish what they need to accomplish to perpetuate the organization.

Superior's Introspection. A man-organization relationship requires the superior to be introspective, too. Suppose he has prided himself on bringing along a bright young man who, he now learns, is thinking of moving into a different field. How can he keep from being angry and disappointed? How can he cope with the conflict when it comes time to make recommendations for advancement or a raise for his protégé?

The superior cannot keep from being angry and disappointed.

Such feelings are natural in such circumstances. He can express his feelings of disappointment to his protégé without being critical of the latter. But, if he continues to feel angry, then he needs to ask himself why another man's assertion of independence irritates him so. The issues of advancement and raises should continue to be based on the same realistic premises as they would have been before.

Of course, it then becomes appropriate for the superior to consider, with the young man, whether—in view of the latter's feelings —he wants to take on the burden of added responsibility and can reasonably discharge it. If he thinks he does and can, he is likely to pursue the new responsibility with added determination. With his occupational choice conflict no longer hidden, and with fewer feelings of guilt about it, his commitment to his chosen alternative is likely to be more intense. And if he has earned a raise, he should get it. For the superior to withhold it would be punishing him, which puts the relationship back on a reward-punishment basis.

The question of how ethical it is to conduct such discussions as part of a business situation hinges on both the climate of the organization and on the sense of personal responsibility of each executive. Where the organization ethos is one of building trust and keeping confidences, there is no reason why executives cannot be as ethical as lawyers or physicians.

If the individual executive cannot be trusted in his relationships with his subordinates, then he cannot have their respect or confidence in any case, and the ordinary MBO appraisal process simply serves as a management pressure device. If the organization ethos is one of rapacious internal competition, backbiting, and distrust, there is little point in talking about self-motivation, human needs, or commitment.

CONCLUSION

Management by objectives and performance appraisal processes, as typically practiced, are inherently self-defeating over the long run because they are based on a reward-punishment psychology that serves to intensify the pressure on the individual while really giving him a very limited choice of objectives. Such processes can be improved by examining the psychological assumptions underlying them, by extending them to include group appraisal and appraisal of superiors by subordinates, and by considering the personal goals of the individual first. These practices require a high level of ethical standards and personal responsibility in the organization.

Employing such appraisal processes would diminish the feeling on the part of the superior that appraisal is a hostile, destructive act. While he and his subordinates would still have to judge the latter's individual performance, this judgment would occur in a context of continuing consideration for personal needs and reappraisal of organizational and environmental realities.

Not having to be continuously on the defensive or constantly aware of the organization's genuine interest in having him meet his personal goals as well as the organization's goals, a manager would be freer to evaluate himself against what has to be done. Since he would have many additional frames of reference in both horizontal and vertical goal setting, he would no longer need to see himself under appraisal (attack, judgment) as an isolated individual against the system. Furthermore, he would have multiple modes for contributing his own ideas and varied methods for exerting influence upward and horizontally.

In these contexts, too, the manager could raise questions and be concerned about qualitative aspects of performance. Then he, his colleagues, and his superiors could together act to cope with such issues without the barrier of having to consider only statistics. Thus a continuing process of interchange would counteract the problem of the static job description and provide multiple avenues for feedback on performance and joint action.

In such an organizational climate, work relationships would then become dynamic networks for both personal and organizational achievements. Not the least of the incidental gain from such arrangements is that problems would more likely be solved spontaneously at the lowest possible levels, which would free superiors simultaneously from the burden of the passed buck and the onus of being the purveyors of hostility.

CHAPTER 7

Psychological Roots of Merger Failures

UP TO THIS POINT, I have been discussing individual and organizational processes as exemplified by middle age and by management by objectives. The psychological man conception transcends either dimension and transcends both in their interaction. The import of the theory can be seen clearly in interorganizational relationships and specifically in merger. In merger one sees unfolding, maturing organisms—this time organizations—interacting with other organizations in the context of varied ego ideals and correspondingly varied self-images. Again, as in earlier discussion, the issues are more clearly seen in instances of failure. I therefore turn to merger failures as the phenomenon through which these issues may be magnified for examination.

Caught up in all the hoopla and glamor that have characterized the great merger spree in recent years, business executives have been preoccupied with the strategies, tactics, and techniques of acquiring, merging, and selling. Yet, frequently the really crucial factor, people, has been superficially dealt with. Nowhere is this shallowness more evident than in those mergers that have been outright mistakes ending with destructive consequences for both parties. Such failures have usually been attributed to rational, technical problems.

I contend, however, that the unrecognized psychological problems, often heavily weighted by fear and obsolescence, are the real culprits and lead to attitudes that are expressed by words like these: "We're smarter and better than they are. After all, we're buying them." "We've got to control them. They need our managerial know-how." "They're out to get all they can from us. They want to be free to do things their own way, but they don't want to be responsible for the results."

Such condescending attitudes on the part of the acquiring organization lead to efforts at manipulation and control that, in turn, produce disillusionment, disappointment, and a feeling of desertion by the smaller company. Loss of morale, personnel, and profits soon follow. This is not to say that all mergers that fail do so for these psychological reasons. Obviously, in some cases sheer incompatibility or the unwillingness of the junior partner to cooperate is more than a rationalization.

In this chapter, I shall examine some of the psychological shoals and suggest ways of avoiding them. Since the trend toward mergers is not likely to abate in the near future, it will become increasingly important to consider carefully how mergers might be handled with greater mutual satisfaction and success.

First, however, let me acknowledge that many mergers have been mutually advantageous to both parties. Thus my focus here—from the perspective of the dominant partner—is, as I noted before, on the many that have been mutually disappointing.[1]

PSYCHOLOGICAL SHOALS

Any discussion of the failures of mergers rightfully begins with the question: Why merge? There are, of course, many important reasons for merging. There are valid economic considerations: to acquire access to more capital, better professional management, or greater product and technical sophistication; to meet competition more effectively; to acquire new products or round out an existing product line; to acquire innovative capacity or tax benefits; to foster growth; and so on. There are also many personal reasons for merging: to realize capital gains or protect an estate; to assure the continuity of an organization; to demonstrate one's managerial or financial competence or both; to become the chief executive officer of a larger organization; and so forth.

---

[1] See, for example, Frederick Wright Searby, "Control Postmerger Change," *Harvard Business Review* (September–October 1969), p. 4.

Unrecognized Motives

Between the lines of these rational reasons for acquisition, there often are two more subtle reasons that are rarely discussed in these terms: *fear* and *obsolescence*. These unrecognized conditions constitute psychological traps because they lead to impulsive actions that compound the very problems that a merger is intended to resolve.

Fear. One pressing wish to merge derives from the feeling that unless the company grows, larger companies will destroy it. Following this logic, destruction is to be avoided only by becoming more powerful. And the fastest way to become more powerful is to buy other, smaller companies and expand.

This attitude then sets in motion a process of accretion, and I use the word advisedly, for the process is psychologically similar to that of a man who seeks to become bigger by becoming fatter. Such a man eats too much because unconsciously he is afraid of being so little. He has a self-image of impotence. There is much folk wisdom to the saying that beneath the bulk of the fat man is hidden a tiny one. While the fat man may be physically large to begin with, he perceives himself to be small for many unconscious reasons and acts accordingly.

So it is with organizations. The initial size of the company may make little difference in this feeling on the part of those in the positions of leadership. The important point is that they feel threatened.

But one of the problems generated by getting bigger by accretion, whether it happens to an individual or an organization, is the loss of flexibility and the additional burdens on the internal systems. More than one organization has found itself bigger and with more managerial problems but with few—if indeed any—long-term gains to show in, say, earnings per share or innovation.

Obsolescence. As organizations age, they develop bureaucratic tendencies and become more rigidly systematic in the way they define jobs, delineate objectives, and narrow task focus and responsibility. The more rigidly the system functions as a system—that is, the better the way in which matters are measured, counted, and controlled—the less room there is for individual initiative and spontaneity. In fact, the purpose of increasing the bureaucratic aspects of the system is to reduce individual variation and to foster known, standard modes of action.

Inevitably, organizations, like aging people, become more stereotyped in their ways, less adaptable to changing conditions, and less flexible in their efforts to cope with their environments. In a word, they become obsolescent. The executives, too, become obsolescent. One way of obtaining enterprising new blood, they decide, is to buy an enterprising organization.

All well and good, but behind the two conditions of fear and obsolescence there frequently are underlying unconscious attitudes that are the actual destructive forces. When one is fearful, his first unconscious step in fighting fear is to deny his fear and tighten up. The word "uptight" aptly characterizes this feeling. When one becomes obsolescent, he tends to adopt a defensive attitude of superiority and to reintensify his customary efforts. The fact that he is the dominant party, together with his denial of fear and his air of superiority, leads to the kinds of condescending attitudes discussed in the early part of this chapter.

CONTROLLING BEHAVIOR

Condescending attitudes lead to behavior that implements them. The attitudes of top management are taken for gospel by staff people, who concretize them into practice. Thus the pivotal issue becomes one of controls. The acquiring organization must, they argue, have the same processes and precedures in all of its components. The newly merged smaller organization must serve the system. Ergo, no sooner bought than controlled.

As the acquiring organization imposes control systems from its established bureaucracy, it stifles in the acquired the very quality it sought to obtain and the larger one becomes even more obsolete. The very words "control" and "controller" specify the problem. They assume by definition that someone must police, ride herd, and keep people in some kind of confinement.

Some managements from the very beginning intend to impose controls and to make arbitrary changes in keeping with their own ways of doing business. However, they never convey such thinking to a prospective merger partner because they know the prospect would hardly be likely to merge under those circumstances. Thus they begin by wooing the prospect, promising him they will change nothing. When the merger is sealed, the original intentions are acted on, and the new partner feels he has been "conned." The underlying contempt of the senior partner for the junior one becomes magnified; the junior now feels he has let himself be taken in.

Perpetuation Problem

Fundamentally, the problem to be dealt with in a merger is the same task every organization always has, namely, to build in perpetuation. This means that from the beginning of the relationship it is essential to create conditions conducive to perpetuation and to develop the capacity in people to assume responsibility.[2] If perpetuation is the basic focus, then control systems and modes of management must foster that intent. If, however, the basic focus is "How do I control the new organization?" then the control devices become the overriding concern. The method is rational; its purpose, fine; and its outcome, efficient control. Therefore, it *should* work. Only when it does not, do people begin to ask questions, and then they usually project solutions which fail to fit the problem: higher salaries, profit sharing, competition, and so forth.

I have no brief against controls or controllers per se, but every form of control, like every other managerial process, is based on some implicit conception of motivation. A control system based on policing assumes people must be whipped into shape and kept there by an "overseer." It conveys to the people who are controlled that they are regarded as inadequate and incompetent and therefore are not to be trusted. Contrast this with a conception of accounting data as feedback on performance by which the people can control their own behavior. The person (or department) that furnishes such information might better be called a "facilitator" and the service stance that goes with it, "facilitating"—provided that is what is really done.

"Family" Integration

From a psychological point of view, the phenomenon of merger is similar to forming a new family. From the acquiring organization's point of view, it is much alike adopting a foster child. From the other point of view, it is akin to getting a stepfather.

---

[2] See Harry Levinson, *The Exceptional Executive* (Cambridge, Mass.: Harvard University Press, 1968).

If the parent is concerned with how to make his child good, he will concentrate on goodness at the expense of the child's development. If he is concerned with rearing the most mature, most capable, most flexible child, then he must be concerned with facilitation of growth, not with control.

This is not to say that controls are bad. To be sure, all children need to be controlled and to learn self-control. Rather, it is to say that when control is the purpose, the whole point is missed. The result is a blob of human clay instead of a living being. Clay may respond to someone else's manipulation; it has no growth potential.

Furthermore, the stepfather who assumes he is going to have to beat the child into shape is in for a running battle. The child will feel deserted and betrayed by the stepfather who promised him affectionate esteem. He will fight if he can, withdraw in anger if he cannot, and leave the family at the first opportunity. So it is with merged managements and even line executives. Suddenly, the dominant management finds itself without those very innovative men it thought it had acquired.

In many mergers, therefore, one finds organizations left with the hollow shells of the name and structure of the acquired company faced with the necessity of bringing in a completely new management group. However, the kinds of managers brought in as replacements will tend to be more bureaucratic or "take charge" types. They are unlikely to be people who have started organizations themselves or who have established records of imaginative innovation.

If those in the merged junior company, assuming it was an innovative organization, joined it because either they could not work under more bureaucratic controls in the first place or such controls inhibited their creativity, they will now feel as though someone were always looking over their shoulders or as if they had become puppets. Even if they remain, they will no longer trust the organization or its leadership. They will spend the rest of their careers there simply going through the motions. Some, with their backs up, will have to be fired or retired early, while others will have to be placed on some innocuous managerial shelf.

I have observed organizations, even as long as 20 years after a merger, in which there was still residual anger at being taken over. Some employees who had been members of the acquired company were still idealizing the old company and comparing the "new" unfavorably with their former circumstances. In their view, everything had been so much better before.

A Case Example

The following case is a typical example of an outcome that was not what the acquiring organization intended. It illustrates that, however rationalized, control focus on the part of the parent organization is essentially self-defeating.

> A small scientific organization, which had operated with relative success in its own naive way—because its scientists and technicians were free to be innovative—was acquired by a larger company. The major stockholders of the small organization wanted to realize capital gains and long-term appreciation. The purchasing corporation wanted to diversify.
>
> Following the merger, the management of the dominant company discovered that the smaller company's financial picture was not as good as it had thought. The immediate response to this discovery was quick imposition of controls by a new take-charge president who had demonstrated previous success in salvaging financially losing situations. He imposed all of the usual textbook methods and standards on his new organization, and he promptly began to lose its key people.
>
> Fortunately in this case, he was quick to call for help. Then, to work the situation through, he shifted from trying to control the new people to facing them with the realities of what the organization was up against.
>
> Knowing what they faced and being responsible people, they dug in and brought the company back into the black. The realities of their financial circumstances were control enough; they did not need a whip.

What about the parent organization's leaders in such a situation? They had the fantasy that *everything* would go up—sales, rate of return, profits. They fully expected that the people in the smaller organization would love them for being merged into their larger, more protective nest with its greater advancement opportunities. They were disillusioned, angry, and frustrated when the opposite occurred. After all, they were not ogres—or were they? If not, then why did people desert them when they were only trying to do what was right to save the smaller organization from its own follies?[3]

MANIPULATION OF PERSONNEL

Although there have always been mergers (the usual practice has been simply to incorporate one company within the other) where little thought has been given to the consequences, this is no longer advisable. When organizations merged, say, 25 or 30 years ago, people stayed, even if they did not like the new parent company. Furthermore, most jobs were routine and promised to remain that way, even at the middle- and upper-management levels.

Today, the traditional, heavily dependent employee-management relationship based on loyalty and long service is outmoded. Competence alone counts.[4] If there is competence in the junior organization, no management can afford to squeeze it out by doing what it did years ago. If it does, it denies people's expectations about gaining greater opportunity out of the merger in terms of their growth and development, their responsibility, and their advancement.

What one needs, in contrast to the stability of a pre-World War II organization, is flexibility and adaptability, which require adaptive, innovative people and a context in which they can solve problems.

Identification Crisis

There is an additional factor to be dealt with, which I call the "identification crisis." In earlier years, employees were less likely to feel it was "their" organization. It was clearly the boss's organization, and they were seen by him all too often as chattels. In more recent times, managements have gone to great lengths to integrate employees as members of the corporate family, to encourage them to identify themselves with the organization, and to see it as their own.[5]

Even when people felt that the organization belonged to the boss, they had some sense of obligation to him. Later, that obligation was reinforced by paternalism. Now, with dispersed ownership, there is

---

[3] See Richard E. Davis, "Compatibility in Corporate Marriages," *Harvard Business Review* (July–August 1968), p. 86.

[4] See Harry Levinson, *Executive Stress* (New York: Harper & Row, 1970), Chapter 19.

[5] See Harry Levinson, *The Exceptional Executive*, Chapter 2.

less likely to be feelings of obligation and loyalty, and merger undermines these feelings even more. In fact, the stronger the identification, the greater the possibility of that feeling of being deserted when merger takes place.

One response to this is mobility. People begin to look for the best "other pastures" break. Newspaper articles report "floating middle management," and too many good executives are spontaneously retiring early to the dismay of their superiors. There are two problems with this phenomenon:

(1) With the decreasing age of company presidents, the potential for mobility declines earlier, so organizations tend to retain people who cannot move but who also have no enthusiasm. This means many hit a plateau. It also means much disillusionment in the very people who should be making contributions. When people do move, largely because they feel hemmed in or without challenge, they are saying, at the most elementary level, "The organization doesn't love me. It doesn't use my talents. It uses me as an expendable device."

(2) There is need for continuous reorganization and regrouping to maintain flexibility in order to cope more easily with new problems. Regrouping is harder when people basically cannot trust the organization. No matter what work groups people find themselves in, the basic identification must be with the organization, or there is no organization.

Vicious Circle

When managements do not see their own tacit con game assumptions—the product of their trying to "sell" the other party, and their own fears—they are left to suffer the consequences without understanding why they occurred. Manipulation as a technique suffers from the fact that it always carries the seeds of its own destruction.

For some organizations, this process has now reached frightening proportions. They buy other companies, impose controls, lose key managers, put in a new leadership group, lose innovative capacity, and then go out to buy more to make up for the new burdens. This vicious circle hinges on an underlying fallacy: controls *produce* profits. Controls are necessary for guidance. When they become the major method of staying profitable, they eventually become self-defeating.

Profitability and survivability derive in the last analysis from adaption to the marketplace. The greater the attention management directs inwardly on the organization, the less attention it gives to the outside world. People become preoccupied with contemplating their own navels. They are taught to beat themselves, to go on economic diets.

To be sure, contemplation and control are highly important, but such self-preoccupation is more characteristic of monks than merchants. Self-flagellation is no substitute for innovative imagination and the aggressive pursuit of those dreams. By the time all the internal squeezing is done, whatever the temporary contribution to profits, skill in coping with the outside is lost. To make matters worse, people feel driven. Morale declines. People feel that no one cares and that they are working only for the dollar. Ultimate financial objectives are seriously threatened.

Some organizations can get away with the manipulation process for a long time—squeezing cash reserves, manipulating accounting methods, selling off less profitable units, and so on. Large organizations with assured resources—like banks, insurance companies, and public utilities—can continue for many years unaware of their losses. But even the largest manufacturing organizations are now having difficulty, as repeated complaints about quality control testify, and the largest financial institutions are having difficulty hiring young people; in addition, they have already been outflanked by newer types of financial organizations.

Reality Gap

Fundamentally, the problem is: What does the president of the organization want? If he wants to evolve a more adaptive organization, he can't get there by the usual means which executives have been following. If he merely wants to be a big man and is not concerned about the price, then he is like the man who does not care about his family so long as he gets the income.

How does such a problem come about? Why is there such a gap between the "real" and the psychological? Why is it so difficult to reconcile the two?

The business executive is fundamentally a rationalist. He is heavily trained in business methods and economic logic. He is largely unaware of the fact that with every technique or process he uses—whether or not it is rational in its own right—he is making an assumption about motivation. The problem is that his assumptions often do not reflect people's actual motivations and feelings.

While it is true *theoretically* that the shortest mathematical distance between two points is a straight line, it is equally true *practically* that while the shortest distance, in terms of time, between two points may be a superhighway, one may have to make many circles in order to get on it. When it comes to matters psychological, all too often the executive is unwilling to make the necessary circles. He thinks he is more practical and direct when he does not; but he is neither, as indicated by repetitive efforts to solve the same old problems.

The self-defined realist equates "real" with palpable, material, measurable, and visible. That which is more subtle is to him "unreal" and therefore easily disregarded. But that is like trying to treat polio only with warm baths or external medication. The executive, like the physician, must evolve ways of seeing that which is not readily visible to the naked eye and of grasping its reality.

There are other reasons for the gap between the real and the psychological. Executives as a breed tend to run scared. They are continuously trying to "make it." They fear failure. In addition, they feel themselves to be under tremendous pressure for results by forces outside themselves. They feel they must respond fast and on the basis of hard facts. As a result, they have not learned to delay action long enough to think about its psychological meaning. They tend to look on such considerations as a luxury they cannot afford.

MINIMIZING THE IMPACT

There are, then, two major problems to be dealt with: (1) the executive's anxieties, and (2) the meshing of two organizations into one so that the marriage yields a family and not merely an association of convenience. Obviously, there are problems in all mergers, as in all marriages. The concern is not to eliminate all problems. Rather, it is to make the choices more rational and the modes for coping with the problems more effective. The following four suggestions should be helpful in minimizing the negative psychological impact of mergers.

Introspective Assessment

Every management that is thinking of buying up another company should ask itself seriously why it is doing so. "Of course," you say, "every management does just that." It does—it asks itself about everything except the psychological issues in the situation. While much thinking goes into the financial and marketing analyses and into evaluating the managerial and product potentials of the organization to be acquired, almost never does the same kind of thinking extend to introspection, particularly with respect to such issues as aspirations, fears, and wishes for power.

After determining why it really wants to merge, every management should then ask itself if it wants to merge for the wrong reasons. If it wants simply to get bigger, out of fear, is fear alone a sufficient motivation? Are there not more rational ways to deal with fear? How rational is the fear? How much of a panic psychology is being played out? If the motivation is fear, then that underlying pressure is likely to continue, resulting in the whipping of the smaller organization and thereby in destroying the very goal management wants to attain. If the motivation is to add zest to a sluggish organization, is it not more reasonable to rejuvenate the old one than to fight obsolescence by merger?

Projected Assumptions

Having assessed its own motivation, the prospective parent organization should next ask itself what assumptions it is making about the other organization. It can infer these from its attitudes toward the other firm and what it is keeping to itself for fear that the other will refuse to merge if all of the intentions are clear. How are these assumptions likely to get management into trouble?

The prospective parent organization must take an honest look at its own control intentions and—beneath those—its assumptions about its projected partners (read "subordinates" instead of "partners" to understand the unconscious motivation better). If the parent management follows the strategy that it will persuade or sweet-talk the other president into merging and that, afterwards, it will show him what *real* management is, it is laying the groundwork for its own failure. Such an attitude is often found when the junior company has behavioral flexibility—such as dress and time freedoms—that is unacceptable to the senior organization.

If the assumption could be put into words, it might go something like this: "You crazy scientists who won't come to work on time, we'll show you." Behind such a statement would be the anger of the parent company toward the other for its success in spite of being so crazy, anger about being dependent on such a type of organization, and anger over the need to prove itself better than the other in order to justify its own existence.

If a management has such feelings, it would do well to examine them critically. Why have such feelings? How justified are they? What will happen if they are sprung after the merger is made? What resentment and resistance will follow? What will be the cost of the consequences?

Organizational Pulse

If management is going to make an assessment of a company that looks attractive, in addition to assessing financial, marketing, and management talent, it should ask itself what the other company is all about psychologically. Why are those people there? Why are they together? What gratifications are they getting? What is their perceived image of themselves? What is their feeling about the organization of which they are a part? Management should not stop with the top executive structure. How do lower level people feel about those issues? Management will have to live with them, too. This does not necessarily mean taking an opinion survey of the whole organization or talking to each individual.

For instance, in the small scientific organization I cited earlier in the case example, turnover at both managerial and worker levels was very low despite the fact that similar companies were paying higher salaries. This suggests that something was holding those people together; if it had held them together over a long period of time while others nearby were earning more, it constituted a psychological cement.

However, the purchaser failed to examine and take seriously the basis of that solidarity. When he failed to recognize the underlying value system and sense of common purpose and, instead, tried to institute seemingly rational managerial goals and controls, he chipped away some of the psychological cement and the whole organization began to crumble.

One can sense the pulse of an organization very easily by the spirit of its people, the way they talk to each other, what they talk about, and their attitude toward strangers. If the plant abruptly shuts down cold and tight for a coffee break—regardless of work in process—and if the people rush madly for the door at quitting time, these can be seen as elementary signals of how people feel about their work, here, negatively.

Part of the problem is that organizations try to be too rational about the things they can measure. Most of the critical elements of an organization being acquired have to do with people's feelings, and these are not so easily measured. Most executives will say, "Yes, I know feelings are important," and then promptly go about disregarding them.

Harmonious Atmosphere

Having assessed some of the feelings of the junior organization, what are the differences between the way *those* people feel about their organization and the tenor and tempo of the prospective parent organization? This is not to say which one is right, but only to ask, "How do they differ?" A hard-nosed, no-nonsense, high-pressure sales organization will have a difficult time assimilating one that depends heavily on service and customer consideration. This is one of the critical points at which a clash is likely to arise.

At the bargaining table, the prospective partners would do well to indicate to each other what they wish from the merger, how they see each other's organizations, how they feel about apparent differences, and how important those differences are to them. In particular, both organizations should be able to answer with psychological honesty, "What does he want me for, really?" Then the prospective partners can jointly evolve their modes of compromise and integration. Such a process also creates a mechanism for the continuing solution of problems as they subsequently arise.

All organizations need devices for solving problems at critical integration points.[6] This is as true for organizations that merge as it is for

---

[6] See Paul R. Lawrence and Jay W. Lorsch, *Organization and Environment* (Boston:

divisions or units within a company. For example, the personnel department of the smaller organization, which may have had certain ways of doing things in response to its top management, now has to deal with the personnel department of the larger organization as well.

How are such issues to be resolved with mutual satisfaction? How are future issues to be confronted? The larger organization must be able to hear the anxieties and pains of the smaller. Where does it hurt as a result of this merger, or where is it likely to hurt?

Most organizations woo the other, persuade it, effect the merger, and then go about business as usual—their way. This is often further compounded when the negotiations are first carried on between presidents, and the president of the smaller organization is assigned to report to a vice president of the larger one. Here is what usually happens:

The vice president, responding to the demands of his own boss for greater control, profitability, and productivity, in turn makes similar demands on the president of the smaller company. The latter now has to deal with his feelings of being deserted, in addition to whatever feelings he may have about being conned and taken over. These feelings may become more acute when whatever he wants to try innovatively is now squashed by fiat from someone he did not bargain for, and with, in the first place. His one channel, short of pounding the table or quitting, is through the man to whom he is reporting.

With these contemporary events, there is a growing general feeling that expectations in mergers are not being fulfilled. This feeling may in turn make it more difficult to consummate mergers as time goes by. Even worse, people may enter mergers as a good many enter marriages these days: "I'll take a chance, and if it doesn't work, I'll leave." That kind of tentative commitment inevitably undermines a marriage; it will inevitably undermine a merger. It usually means that the relationship is bound by various secret clauses and reservations, as well as hidden expectations, which then continually burden both parties.

Complicating these forces is an increasing frequency of feelings of

Harvard University Graduate School of Business Administration, Division of Research, 1967).

guilt on the part of presidents who sell out after having built organizations that are loyal to them. The long-term identification is exploited by the senior organization, control modes are introduced, procedures are changed arbitrarily, and the cohesive organization, with the close relationships people had with each other, now becomes just another place to work.

In such cases, people have learned an important lesson: it does not pay to be loyal, to identify, to invest themselves in an organization or its leadership. They will be sold down the river.

The old presidents are then angry with themselves for what they have done and communicate this anger to others who may be in the same position. The old presidents fight as long as they can, but ultimately quit or are eased out. They are left with residual feelings of anger, guilt, and resentment, and the depression that follows.

Of course, many presidents will disregard such experiences. They are like middle-aged maiden ladies still looking for a husband for security. They are prone to take whatever comes along, later finding the price too high to pay, and, subsequently, seeking ways out.

Thus it is important not to try to con the junior organization's managers. The senior partner may buy them, but it will also, eventually, lose them. Even if the senior partner acquires the people, the products, and the plants, it will have unwilling, resentful partners who feel they have been taken. They will buck every way they can, and the senior partner will have lost their trust permanently.

The dominant management needs to be as straight and as factual as it can and not withhold information about what it plans to do. It will only be kidding itself. In fact, the senior partner would do well to let the junior's managers examine its own organization and talk to a wide range of its people. Above all, management should never promise more than it can deliver. That is a business failing. For example, many organizations these days are promising young people creative possibilities, but most are not organized to permit such innovation. They therefore get rapid turnover and mutual disillusionment. Who needs it?

A contemporary example of this fourth suggestion being put into practice, at least according to a published account,[7] was the merger

---

[7] Chris Welles, "The Battle for United Fruit," *Investment Banking and Corporate Financing* (Spring 1969), p. 27.

of AMK and United Fruit. Eli M. Black, president and board chairman of AMK (now United Brands), it is reported, operates with the philosophy that the best way to win such a company is to win its management. After proffering the merger, Black told John M. Fox, then board chairman of United Fruit, that he would make no further moves toward gaining control without the approval of United Fruit's management. There would be no raids, no end runs, no fights. AMK wanted only a minority position, not control, on the UF board.

The two managements met daily during the negotiating process, and Black invited the UF management to visit AMK in New York. Black's whole concern was to create an atmosphere of harmony and rapport. In that he succeeded, for, according to Fox, "Black never went back or changed a single thing he had promised us. He never acted without consulting us. He lived up to his word."

CONCLUSION

There are many reasons for merger, including psychological ones. Many mergers have been disappointing in their results and painful to their participants. These failures have been attributed largely to rational, financial, economic, and managerial problems.

I contend that some psychological reasons for merger not only constitute a major, if unrecognized, force toward merger, but that they also constitute the basis for many, if not most, disappointments and failures. At least those that have turned sour, or have the most dangerous potential for turning sour, are those that arise out of fear, leading to some neurotic wish to become big by voraciously gobbling up others, or out of obsolescence.

Such mergers flounder because of the hidden assumptions the senior partner makes and the condescending attitudes toward the junior organization which then follow. These result in efforts at manipulation and control that, in turn, produce (1) disillusionment and the feeling of desertion on the part of the junior organization, and (2) disappointment, loss of personnel, and declining profitability for the dominant organization.

To cope with these issues, I have suggested that senior executives of the dominant company should

Probe their own motivations for merging.

Review the psychological assumptions that they have about the other party in the merger.

Assess the psychological relationships and attitudes of the people in the junior organization and note how they may differ from those in the senior organization.

Out of open, honest discussion of these motivations, assumptions, and differences, create a harmonious atmosphere in which problem-solving mechanisms are set up so that the anguish of the junior organization can be heard and acted on and so operating modes can be evolved rather than imposed.

These suggestions depend for their validity on the recognition of the reality and power of feelings and, particularly, on the fact that both the senior and the junior organization will be equal in psychological power despite vast differences in economic power. Either the senior management understands the psychological power of its partner and acts accordingly, or it stands to lose what it sought in the merger.

The importance of these considerations goes beyond corporations per se. If contemporary modes of merger result in widespread loss of initiative, increased constriction of imagination, and floating populations of executives, this has not only self-defeating implications for organizations but also has powerful negative effects on society.

CHAPTER 8

Conflicts That Plague Family Businesses

THE TENSION BETWEEN AFFECTION AND AGGRESSION as concurrent operating feelings, compounded by dependency and mastery strivings, is most obvious in those situations where people grow and develop together. This is especially true where there are sharp differences of power which require one to seek the approval of the other, to lean more heavily on the other, and to express rivalry and hostility in more covert form. Family businesses are the ideal medium for viewing these issues. Once again, I am making an abrupt turn from interorganizational processes to intraorganizational behavior, where the organization itself takes on special meaning for the people who are involved in it, particularly with reference to the evolution and maintenance of the self-image. In addition, there is no better instrumentality for viewing the business as a recapitulation of the family structure than a family business.

The most successful business executives often are men who have built their own companies. Ironically, their very success frequently brings to them and members of their families personal problems of an intensity rarely encountered by professional managers. And these problems make family businesses possibly the most difficult to operate.[1]

It is obvious common sense that when managerial decisions are in-

---

[1] For two thoughtful views of the subject, see Robert G. Donnelley, "The Family Business," *Harvard Business Review* (July–August 1964), p. 93; Seymour Tilles, "Survival Strategies for Family Firms," *European Business* (April 1970), p. 9.

fluenced by feelings about and responsibilities toward relatives in the business, when nepotism exerts a negative influence, and when a company is run more to honor a family tradition than for its own needs and purposes, there is likely to be trouble. However, the problems of family businesses go considerably deeper than those issues. In this chapter I shall examine some of the more difficult underlying psychological elements in operating such businesses and suggest some ways of coping with them.

THEY START WITH THE FOUNDER

The difficulties of the family business begin with the founder. Usually he is an entrepreneur for whom the business has at least three important meanings.

(1) Research evidence indicates that the entrepreneur characteristically has unresolved conflicts with his father. He is therefore uncomfortable when being supervised and starts his own business, both to outdo his father and to escape the authority and rivalry of more powerful figures.[2]

(2) An entrepreneur's business is simultaneously his "baby" and his "mistress." Those who work with him and for him are characteristically his instruments in the process of shaping the organization. If any among them aspires to be other than a device for the founder—that is, if he wants to acquire power himself—he is soon likely to find himself on the outside looking in. This is the reason why so many organizations decline when their founders age or die.

(3) For the entrepreneur, the business is essentially an extension of himself, a medium for his personal gratification and achievement above all. And if he is concerned about what happens to his business after he passes on, that concern usually takes the form of thinking about the kind of monument he will leave behind.

RIVALRY

The fundamental psychological conflict in family businesses is rivalry, compounded by feelings of guilt, when more than one family member is involved. The rivalry may be felt by the founder—even though no relatives are in the business—when he unconsciously

---

[2] See Orvis F. Collins, David G. Moore, and Darab B. Unwalla, *The Enterprising Man* (East Lansing: Michigan State University Bureau of Business Research, 1964).

senses (justifiably or not) that subordinates are threatening to remove him from his center of power. Consider the following case example.

> An entrepreneur, whose organization makes scientific equipment and bears his name, has built a sizable enterprise in international markets. He has said that he wants his company to be noted all over the world for contributing to society. He has attracted many young men with the promise of rapid promotions, but he guarantees their failure by giving them assignments and then turning them loose without adequate organizational support. He intrudes into the young men's decision making, but he counterbalances this behavior with paternalistic devices. (His company provides employees with more benefits than any other I have known.) This technique makes his subordinates angry at him for what he has done, then angry at themselves for being hostile to such a kind man. Ultimately, it makes them feel utterly inadequate. He can get people to take responsibility and move up into executive positions, but his behavior has made certain that he will never have a rival.

The conflicts created by rivalries among family members—between fathers and sons, among brothers, and between executives and other relatives—have a chronically abrasive effect on the principals. Those family members in the business must face up to the impact that these relationships exert and must learn to deal with them, not only for their own emotional health but for the welfare of the business as well.

Father-Son Rivalry

As I have indicated, for the founder the business is an instrument, an extension of himself. So he has great difficulty giving up his baby, his mistress, his instrument, his source of social power, or whatever else the business may mean to him. Characteristically, he has great difficulty delegating authority, and he most usually refuses to retire despite repeated promises to do so. This behavior has certain implications for father-son relationships. While he consciously wishes to pass his business on to his son and also wants him to attain his place in the sun, unconsciously the father feels that to yield the business would be to lose his masculinity. At the same time, and also unconsciously, he needs to continue to demonstrate his own competence. That is, he must constantly reassure himself that he alone is competent to make "his" organization succeed. Unconsciously the father does not want his son to win, take away his combination baby and mistress, and displace him from his summit position. These conflicting emotions cause the father to behave in an inexplicable and contradictory manner, leading those close to him to think that while on the one hand he wants the business to succeed, on the other hand he is determined to make it fail.

The son's feelings of rivalry are a reflection of his father's. The son naturally seeks increasing responsibility commensurate with his growing maturity and wants the freedom to act responsibly on his own. But he is frustrated by his father's intrusions, broken promises of retirement, and self-aggrandizement. The son resents being kept in an infantile role—always the little boy in his father's eyes—with the accompanying contempt, condescension, and lack of confidence that, in such a situation, frequently characterize the father's attitude. The son also resents remaining dependent on his father for his income level and, as often, for title, office, promotion, and the other usual perquisites of an executive. The father's erratic and unpredictable behavior in these matters makes this dependency more unpalatable.

I have observed a number of such men who, even as company presidents, are still being victimized by their fathers who remain chairmen of the board and chief executive officers.

"Why Don't You Let Me Grow Up?" Characteristically, fathers and sons, particularly the latter, are terribly torn by these conflicts; the father looks on the son as ungrateful and unappreciative, and the son feels both hostile to his father and guilty for his hostility. The father bears the feeling that the son never will be man enough to run the business, but he tries to hide that feeling from his son. The son yearns for his chance to run it and waits impatiently but still loyally in the wings—often for years beyond the age when others in nonfamily organizations normally take executive responsibility—for his place on the stage.

If the pressures become so severe for the son that he thinks of leaving, he feels disloyal but at the same time fears losing the opportunity that would be his if he could only wait a little longer. He defers his anticipated gratification and pleasure; but, with each postponement, his anger, disappointment, frustration, and tension mount. The following case is a typical situation.

Matthew Anderson, a man who founded a reclaimed-metals business, has two sons. John, the elder, is his logical successor; but Anderson has given him little freedom to act independently, pointing out that, despite limited education, he (the father) has built the business and intuitively knows more about how to make it successful. Though he has told John that he wants him to be a partner, he treats John more like a flunky than an executive, let alone a successor. He pays the elder son a small salary, always with the excuse that he should not expect more because someday he will inherit the business. He grants minimal raises sporadically, never recognizing John's need to support his family in a style fitting his position in the company.

When John once protested and demanded more responsibility and more income, his father gave Henry, the second son, a vice presidential title and a higher income. When Henry asked for greater freedom and responsibility, Anderson turned back to John and made him president (in name only). The father, as chairman of the board and chief executive officer, continued to second-guess John, excluded Henry from conferences (which of course increased John's feelings of guilt), and told John that Henry was "no good" and could not run the business.

Later, when John sought to develop new aspects of the business to avoid the fluctuations of the metals market, his father vetoed the ideas, saying, "This is what we know, and this is what we are going to do." He failed to see the possible destructive effects of market cycles on fixed overhead costs and the potential inroads of plastics and other cheaper materials on the reclaimed-metals business. The upshot was that profits declined and the business became more vulnerable to both domestic and foreign (particularly Japanese) competition. When John argued with his father about this, he got the response: "What do you know? You're still green. I went through the Depression." Once again Anderson turned to Henry—making the black sheep white, and vice versa. Angered, John decided to quit the business, but his mother said, "You can't leave your father; he needs you." Anderson accused him of being ungrateful, but he also offered to retire, as he had promised to do several times before.

Despite his pain, John could not free himself from his father. (Only an ingrate would desert his father, he told himself.) Also John knew that if he departed, he could not go into competition with his father, because that would destroy him. But John shrank from entering an unfamiliar business. Nevertheless, from time to time John has explored other opportunities while remaining in the business. But each time his father has undercut him. For instance, John once wanted to borrow money for a venture, but Anderson told the bankers that his son was not responsible. Now, when John is middle-aged, he and his father are still battling. In effect John is asking, "Why don't you let me grow up?" and his father is answering, "I'm the only man around here. You must stay here and be my boy."

"He's Destroying the Business." The son also has intense rivalry feelings, of course. These, too, can result in fierce competition with his father and hostile rejection of him or abject dependence on him. Sometimes the competition can lead to a manipulative alignment with the mother against him. Consider the following case.

Bill Margate, a recent business school graduate, knew that he would go into his father's electronic components business. But he decided that he should first get experience elsewhere, so he spent four years with a large manufacturing company. From his education and experience, he became aware of how unsophisticated his father was about running the business and set about showing the senior Margate how a business should be professionally managed.

Margate can do no right in Bill's eyes, at least not according to the books which he has read but which his father has never heard of. Bill frequently criticizes his father, showing him how ignorant he is. When Margate calls his son "green," Bill retorts, "I've forgotten more about managing a business than you'll ever know."

Bill's mother is also involved in the business; she has been at her husband's side for many years, though their relationship is less than the best. Mrs. Margate dotes on her son and complains to him about her husband, and she encourages Bill in his attacks on his father. When Bill undertook several ventures that floundered, she excused the failures as being caused by his father's interference. But whenever the father-son battle reaches a peak, Mrs. Margate shifts allegiance and stands behind her husband. So the senior Margate has an ally when the chips are down, at the price of a constant beating until he gets to that point.

The struggle for the business has remained a stand-off. But as the elder Margate has grown older, his son's attacks have begun to tell on him. Bill has urged him to take long Florida vacations, but Margate refuses because he fears what would happen when his back is turned. For the same reason, he does not permit Bill to sign checks for the company.

Now Margate has become senile, and Bill's criticism of him continues, even in public. "He's destroying the business," Bill will say. However, Bill cannot act appropriately to remove his father (even though he is now incompetent) because of his guilt feelings about his incessant attacks. That would destroy his father, literally, and he cannot bring himself to do it.

"The Old Man Really Built It." The problem for the son becomes especially acute when and if he does take over. Often the father has become obsolete in his managerial conceptions. The organization may have grown beyond one man's capacity to control it effectively. That man may have been a star whose imagination, creativity, or drive are almost impossible to duplicate. He may also have been a charismatic figure with whom employees and even the public identified.

Whatever the combination of factors, the son is likely to have to take over an organization with many weaknesses hidden behind the powerful facade of the departed leader. For these reasons many businesses, at the end of their founders' tenure, fall apart, are pirated, or are merged into other organizations. The Ford Motor Company, at the demise of Henry Ford, was a case in point; a completely new management had to be brought in. Henry Ford II was faced with the uncomfortable task of having to regenerate a company that appeared to have the potential for continued success but which, according to some, could easily have gone bankrupt.

While the son is acting to repair the organizational weaknesses left by his father, he is subject to the criticism of those persons who, envious of his position, are waiting for him to stumble. They "know" that he is not as good as his father. If he does less well than his father, regardless of whether there are unfavorable economic conditions or other causes, he is subject to the charge of having thrown away an opportunity on which others could have capitalized. The scion cannot win. If he takes over a successful enterprise, and even if he makes it much more successful than anyone could have imagined, the onlookers nevertheless stimulate his feelings of inadequacy. They say, "What did you expect? After all, look what he started with." The following case illustrates this.

Tom Schlesinger, the president of a restaurant chain, inherited the business after his father had built a profitable regional network of outlets with a widely known name—a model for the industry. Tom has expanded it into nearly a national operation. He has done this with astute methods of finance that allow great flexibility and with effective control methods that maintain meal quality and at the same time minimize waste. By any standards he has made an important contribution to the business. But those who remember his father cannot see what Tom has done because the aura of his father still remains. They tend to minimize Tom's contribution with such observations as, "Well, you know, the old man really built that business." Tom cannot change the attitude of those who knew his father, and he feels it is important to keep lauding his father's accomplishments in order to present a solid family image to employees, customers, and the community. But he is frustrated because he has no way of getting the world to see how well he has done.

Brother-Brother Rivalry

The father-son rivalry is matched in intensity by the brother-brother rivalry. Their competition may be exacerbated by the father if he tries to play the sons off against each other or has decided that one should wear his mantle, as I discussed previously. (In my experience, the greatest difficulties of this kind occur when there are only two brothers in the organization.) The problem is further complicated if their mother and their wives are also directly or indirectly involved in the business. Mothers have their favorites—regardless of what they say—and each wife, of course, has a stake in her husband's position. He can become a foil for his wife's fantasies and ambition.

The rivalry between brothers for their father's approval, which begins in childhood, continues into adult life. It can reach such an intensity that it colors every management decision and magnifies the jockeying for power that goes on in all organizations. Consider the following situation.

Arthur is president and Warren, five years younger than his brother, is an operating vice president of the medium-sized retailing organization they inherited. To anyone who cares to listen, each maintains that he can get along very well without the other. Arthur insists that Warren is not smart, not as good a businessman as he; that his judgment is bad; and that even if given the chance, he would be unable to manage the business. Warren asserts that when the two were growing up, Arthur considered him to be a competitor, but for his part, he (Warren) did not care to compete because he was younger and smaller. Warren says that he cannot understand why his older brother has always acted as if they were rivals and adds, "I just want a chance to do my thing. If he'd only let me alone with responsibility! But he acts as if the world would fall apart if I had that chance."

Every staff meeting and meeting of the board (which include non-family members) become battles between the brothers. Associates, employees, and friends back off because they decline to take sides. The operation of the organization has been turned into a continuous family conflict.

The Elder . . . Ordinarily, the elder brother succeeds his father. But this custom reaffirms the belief of the younger brother (or brothers) that the oldest is indeed the favorite. In any event, the older brother often has a condescending attitude toward the younger. In their earliest years the older is larger, physically stronger, more competent, and more knowledgeable than the younger merely because of the difference in age, as in the case I just cited.

Only in rare instances does the younger brother have the opportunity to match the skills, competence, and experience of the elder until they reach adulthood. By that time the nature of this relationship is so well established that the older brother has difficulty regarding the younger one as adequate and competent. Moreover, the elder child is earlier and longer in contact with the parents, and their control efforts fall more heavily on him. Consequently, older children tend to develop stronger consciences, drive themselves harder, expect more of themselves, and control themselves more rigidly than younger ones. Being, therefore, already a harsh judge of himself, the elder is likely to be an even harsher judge of his younger siblings.

. . . And the Younger. The younger brother attempts to compensate for the effects of this childhood relationship and his older brother's efforts to control him by trying to carve out a place in the business that is his own. This he guards with great zeal, keeping the older brother out so he can demonstrate to himself, his brother, and others that he is indeed competent and has his own piece of the action for which he is independently responsible.

If the brothers own equal shares in the organization and both are members of the board, as is frequently the case, the problems are compounded. On the board they can argue policy from equally strong positions. However, when they return to operations in which one is subordinate to the other, the subordinate one, usually the junior brother, finds it extremely difficult to think of himself in a subservient role.

The younger one usually is unable to surmount this problem in their mutual relationship. He tends to be less confident than his brother and considers himself to be at a permanent disadvantage, always overcontrolled, always unheeded. Since the older brother views the younger one as being less able, he becomes involved in self-fulfilling prophecies. Distrusting his younger brother, he is likely to overcontrol him, give him less opportunity for freedom and responsibility—which in turn make for maturity and growth—and to reject all signs of the younger brother's increasing competence.

If for some reason the younger brother displaces the older one, and particularly if the latter becomes subordinate to him, the younger brother is faced with feelings of guilt for having attacked the elder and usurped what so often is accepted as the senior brother's rightful role.

INTRAFAMILY FRICTION

The problems of the father and brothers extend to other relatives when they, too, become involved in the business. In some families it is expected that all who wish to join the company will have places there. This can have devastating effects, particularly if the jobs are sinecures.

The chief executive of a family business naturally feels a heavy responsibility for the family fortunes. If he does not produce a profit, the effect on what he considers to be his image in the financial markets may mean less to him than the income reduction that members of his family will suffer. So he is vulnerable to backbiting from persons whom he knows only too well and whom he cannot dismiss as faceless. Consider the following case.

> Three brothers started a knitting business. Only one of the brothers had sons, and only one of those sons stayed in the business; he eventually became president. The stock is held by the family. Two widowed

aunts, his mother, his female cousins (one of whom is already wid-
owed), and his brother, a practicing architect, depend on the business
for significant income.

When business is off, the women complain. If the president wants to
buy more equipment, they resist. If they hear complaints from employees or merchant friends, they make these complaints known at family
gatherings. The president is never free from the vixens who are constantly criticizing and second-guessing him. Perhaps more critical for
the health of the business are the factional divisions that spring up in
the organization as associates and subordinates choose the family members with whom they want to be identified. (Often, however, those who
take sides discover that in a crisis the family unites against "outsiders,"
including their partisans, who are then viewed as trying to divide the
family.)

If the nonfamily employees or board members decide not to become
involved in a family fight and withdraw from relations with its members
until the conflict is resolved, the work of the organization may be para-
lyzed. Worse yet, the dispute may eventually embroil the entire organization, resulting in conflicts at the lowest levels as employees try to
cope with the quarrels thrust on them. Now the business has become a
battleground that produces casualties but no peace. Such internecine
warfare constitutes a tremendous barrier to communication, and frus-
trates adequate planning and rational decision making. A business in
which numerous members of the family of varying ages and relationships are involved often becomes painfully disrupted around issues of
empires and succession. Its units tend to become family-member territories and therefore poorly integrated organizationally, if at all.

As for succession, the dominant or patriarchal leader may fully expect to pass on the mantle of leadership to other, elder relatives in their
turn. He may even promise them leadership roles, particularly if he has
had to develop a coalition to support his position. But for both realistic
and irrational reasons he may well come to feel that none of the family
members is capable of filling the role. He cannot very well disclose his
decision, however, without arousing conflict, and he cannot bring in
outside managers without betraying his relatives or reneging on his
promises. On the other hand, he fears what would happen if he died
without having designated a successor.

He may decide that the only way out is to sell the business (at least
each relative will then get his fair share). But that solution is costly—it
signifies not only the loss of the business as a means of employment but
also the betrayal of a tradition and, inevitably, the dissolution of close

family ties that have been maintained through the medium of the business.

What can be done about these problems?

Most entrepreneurial fathers seem unable to resolve their dilemma themselves. They tend to be rigid and righteous, finding it difficult to understand that there is another, equally valid point of view that they can accept without becoming weaklings. Well-meaning outsiders, who try to help the father see the effects of his behavior and think seriously about succession, usually find themselves rejected. Then they lose whatever beneficial influence they may have had on him.

Several approaches have worked well. In some instances, sons have told their fathers that they recognize how important it is to the father to run his own business, but it is just as important for them to have the opportunity to "do their own thing." They then establish small new ventures, either under the corporate umbrella or outside it, without deserting their father. In a variant of this approach, a father who heads a retail operation opened a store in a different community for each of his sons. They do their buying together, with appropriate variations for each community, and maintain a common name and format, but each son runs his own operation while the father continues to run his. In still another situation, the father merged his company into a larger one. Each of his two sons then became president of a subsidiary, and the father started a new venture while serving as a policy guide to his sons.

The Son's Role

Whether such alternatives can work depends in part on how the son conducts himself. He must be honest with himself and consider his paternal relationship candidly. He must take steps like the following:

(1) The son must ask himself why he chose to go into the family business. Most sons will say it is because of the opportunity and the feelings of guilt if they had not done so. Often, however, the basic reason is that a powerful father has helped make his son dependent on him, and so his son is reluctant to strike out on his own.

The son rationalizes his reluctance on the basis of opportunity and guilt. Struggling with his own dependency, he is more likely to continue to fight his father in the business because he is still trying to escape his father's control.

(2) Having examined this issue, and recognizing whatever validity it may have for him, the son must realize how often his own feelings of rivalry and anger get in his way. The more intense the rivalry, the more determinedly he seeks to push his father from his throne and the more aggressively the latter must defend himself. The son must therefore refrain from attack.

(3) The son must quietly and with dignity, as a mature man, apprise his father of the realities—that he needs an area of freedom and an independent medium to develop skills and responsibilities. He can do so within the company framework or, if that is not feasible, outside it. In his own self-interest, as well as the company's, the son must be certain that he gets the opportunity.

(4) The son must not allow himself to be played off against his brother, and he must not allow his guilt to be manipulated. By the same token, he himself must not become involved with others in manipulation.

(5) The son must honestly recognize and respect his father's achievement and competence. To build a business is no mean task, and usually the father still has useful skills and knowledge. Furthermore, the son should recognize the powerful psychological meaning of the business to his father and not expect him to be rational about his relationship to it.

If the son is still unable to make choices about what he wants to do, then, despite his pain and his father's reluctance to seek help, he himself must do so. Only he can take the initiative to relieve his anguish.

An example of how a group of sons took the initiative is evidenced by a group calling itself SOB's (Sons of Bosses International). The group was formed to encourage men in that position to talk over common problems and share solutions. In addition to educating themselves about the psychological dimensions of their situation, the members make it a practice from time to time to invite their fathers as a group to discuss their mutual problems openly. Fathers and sons also get together separately. This procedure enables fathers and sons to realize that their particular problems are not unique, and helps them to obtain support from those in a similar predicament.

Another approach for a son would be to ask his father to read a particular article and then discuss it privately with a neutral third party of their choice. This would help them to develop a perspective on their feelings and behavior. Having done so, a father is then in a better position to talk with his son, in the presence of the third party. The third person must use his good offices to subdue recrimination. At the same time he must foster the father's expression of his fears over losing control, being unneeded, and suffering rejection, as well as the son's concerns about being overcontrolled, infantilized, and exploited.

If meeting with the third party fails, the next step is consultation with a psychologist or psychiatrist. There are rare instances, usually when conflict becomes severe, in which father and son are willing to go to a professional together or separately. In such cases it is often possible for the father to begin to make compromises, learn to understand his and his son's motivations, and work out with him newly defined, more compatible roles. Usually, however, such an effort requires continued supportive work by the professional and a strong desire on the part of both men to resolve their differences.

If all these measures fail, those who work with patriarchs must learn to tolerate their situation until the opportunity arises for a change.

Fraternal Spirit

With respect to the brother-brother conflict, it is important for brothers to see that in their relationship they recapitulate ancient rivalries, and to perceive clearly the psychological posture each assumes toward the other. Once they understand these two issues, they must talk together about them. They should try to discuss freely the fears, worries, anger, and disappointments caused by each other. They should also be able to talk about their affection for each other.

Since there is love and hate in all relationships, theirs cannot, by definition, be pure. They should not feel guilty about their anger with each other, but they do need to talk it out. Having done that, they then must consider how they can divide the tasks in the organization, so that each will have a chance to acquire and demonstrate competence, and work in a complementary relationship with the other.

A brother cannot easily be subordinate at one level and equal on another. If a brother is an operating executive subordinate to the other, he gets into difficulty when he tries to be an equal on the board of directors. If more than one brother is on the board, then only one, as a rule, should be an operating executive. Of course, such rules are unnecessary if the brothers work well together.

If the brothers still cannot resolve their conflicts, then it becomes necessary to seek professional aid. If that does not help, they should consider being in separate organizations. In such a case, the big problem is the feeling of guilt which the departing brother is likely to have for deserting the other and the family business.

Toward Professional Management

Where there are multiple and complex family relationships and obligations in a company, and particularly problems about succession, the best solution is a transcendent one. The family members should form a trust, taking all the relatives out of business operations while enabling them to continue to act in concert as a family. The trust could allot financial support to every member who desires it to develop new business ventures on behalf of the family, thus providing a business interest that replaces the previous operating activity. This also helps maintain family cohesion and preserve the family's leadership role in the community.

In general, the wisest course for any business, family or nonfamily, is to move to professional management as quickly as possible. Every business must define its overriding purpose for being, from which it derives its objectives. Within this planning framework, the business must have a system for appraising the degree to which it and its components are achieving the goals that have been set.

All organizations need to rear subordinates in a systematic manner, thus creating the basic condition for their own regeneration. I know of no family business capable of sustaining regeneration over the long term solely through the medium of its own family members.

Where there is conflict, or inadequately rationalized territories, members of the family should move up and out of operations as quickly as possible into policy positions. Such movement recognizes the reality of ownership but does not confuse ownership with management. It also provides the opportunity for professionally trained managers to succeed to major operating roles, instead of having to go to other organizations as soon as they are ready for major responsibility. The more competitive the business situation, the more imperative such a succession pattern is.

More than others, the family members need to have their own outside activities from which they can derive gratification equal to what they can obtain in the company. Otherwise they will be unable to let go and will continue to be barriers to others. Moreover, they will make it difficult to recruit and develop young people with leadership potential who, as they mature, will see the inevitable barriers.

A number of family businesses have handled these issues wisely and have become highly professional in their management. The Dayton-Hudson Corporation and E. I. du Pont de Nemours are examples. Family members in both organizations must compete for advancement on the same terms as nonfamily managers. This practice is reinforced, at least at Dayton-Hudson, by a thorough performance appraisal system that includes appraisal of the chairman and president by a committee of the board.

CONCLUSION

It is very difficult to cope with the problems of the family business. That does not mean, however, that one should merely endure them. There is no point in stewing in anger and guilt, since chronic irritation is only self-flagellation. It solves no problems; it only increases anger and hostility and paves the way for explosion, recrimination, and impaired relations.

The family member can do something about such problems, as he can with any other. If reasonable steps to solve the problems do not work and he continues to feel bound to the organization, his problem is largely psychological. To free himself to make choices about what he wants to do, he must talk his feelings out with his rival in the organization, which is best done in the presence of a neutral third person. Sometimes professional help is necessary. This will reduce sufficiently the intensity of the emotions generated by the problem, so that the family member can see possible alternatives more clearly and make choices more freely. That is better than the years of agitation that usually accompany such problems, unless of course the rival needs to expiate his guilt by continuing to punish himself. In that case, it is his problem and not necessarily that of the family business.

CHAPTER 9

Revitalizing a Bureaucracy

THE PSYCHOLOGICAL MAN CONCEPTION can be helpful, not only with respect to people alone and organizations in their interactions with other organizations, but also in terms of thinking about evolving more effective processes of adaptation for both. These issues come to the fore when the need for organizational change arises. A classical example of the requirement for change occurs when a historically bureaucratic organization has to become more adaptively flexible. The fundamental issue in such a change effort relates to the concept of mastery. In historically bureaucratic organizations, where control is the dominant theme, the task is to help people establish more effective control over the system in which they operate as contrasted with being controlled by it.

Such a process of establishing mastery involves not only new forms of organization but also new methods for working together and a new sense of a person's relationship to others and to the organization. It requires a clearer delineation of the organization's tasks and function, a more open and direct confrontation of the problems which the organization experiences, and new avenues for obtaining, processing, and acting on information.

Many organizational change agents and many organizational

AUTHOR'S NOTE: The original version of this paper was written with Chris Petrow and Thomas Stern of the State Department. I have condensed much of their contribution to highlight my own thinking. Neither they nor the Department of State bear any responsibility for this version of our work.

change efforts are based on such conceptions. Many also involve the modal concept of involvement. However, most do not delineate steps based on the developmental readiness of organization members as a group. The psychological man conception, as already indicated, includes a notion of developmental or maturational stages. These hold for organizations as well as for individuals. People in organizations evolve in steps toward more effective mastery, and techniques for helping them do so must take into account readiness for certain steps. Ministration needs, or those for support, are a prerequisite for maturation and ultimately for mastery. In the process described in this chapter, ministration needs are supplied by both organizational leadership and outside consultation, supporting the avenues for maturation and ultimate mastery by the adopted methods. The fulfillment of these needs in sequential and parallel steps enhances the self-image, moves people closer to their ego ideals and the attainment of the organizational ego ideal, and raises self-esteem. Once the sense of competence has been affirmed in this manner, once common bonds around common tasks and interests have been established, once a continuity of relationships and practices directed to defined goals has been confirmed, these then serve as bonds of stability which create the conditions for increasingly open and frank discussion of issues and problem solving and for the management of creative conflict which is a necessary precondition for flexible adaptation.

Organizations, like people, grow old and stale. Bureaucratic organizations are particularly prone to sclerotic processes. Government bureaucracies, undisciplined by a profit motive or the realities of adapting to a competitive market situation, have little stimulus to compel them to function differently, particularly to the extent of adopting more effective management practices. When they develop the sluggishness of aging, no matter how much they are aware of their need to change, they have inadequate mechanisms to do so. Yet change they must. How do you change a bureaucracy?

In this chapter I shall describe how the U.S. Department of State, perhaps the most criticized of the federal government bureaucracies, undertook to change itself in the direction of becoming more effective managerially. I do so in the belief that the logic and process of this change effort might well be usefully adapted by other organizations of all institutional forms—business, church, school, hospital—if the same conditions prevail.

THE MEANING OF BUREAUCRACY

The word "bureaucracy" is much bandied. However, it has specific connotations to those who use the term professionally. These connotations constitute the crux of the problem to be dealt with in change, for they refer to those features that characterize a bureaucracy. There are essentially four major ones.[1]

(1) Impersonal rules strictly delimit and define the tasks of each employee under all job situations.

(2) Decisions which must be made outside of rule prescriptions are highly centralized. They are made at a level distant from the point at which the results are to be implemented.

(3) The organization is structured hierarchically in such a way that the strata, or levels, are isolated from each other. The people in each stratum form peer groups that develop strong norms that control the behavior of their members.

(4) Despite all of the rules, there are a few people at key points who have strategic power because they are in contact with uncertain issues. They have to reduce the ambiguity of those issues so that others may apply their rules and process their work. These people are therefore more powerful than others at the same level. This makes the others more dependent on them and therefore creates conditions for potential conflict.

It is evident that when questions, conflict, or differences arise, more rules will be made and decisions pushed upward. Communications channels will thus be further distended and the system further rigidified. Therefore a bureaucratic organization becomes less flexible in dealing with change by its very efforts to do so.

Although power is concentrated in the top management, the power of the top is significantly limited by the detailed job descriptions and delimitations of function. These are the parameters of the "boxes" on the traditional organization chart. It is difficult for the

---

[1] Michel Crozier, *The Bureaucratic Phenomenon* (Chicago: University of Chicago Press, 1964).

"top" to direct the functions of the "boxes" for their tasks are specialized and frequently require specialized knowledge. The top may change the jobs and functions, but the work must be carried on, so, short of not doing the work, the top can only shuffle it about by reorganization. The boxes remain the same though the incumbents may change. Most organizational change is therefore only a shift of boxes on the organization chart or an alteration of their functions. Soon these new structures become hardened. Besides, to shift one is to affect others. Further, the authority pattern must be preserved to retain any function at all. Certainly there may be some streamlining or reordering of boxes, but as already indicated, the *adaptive capacity* of the organization is little changed despite the "new look," "the fresh breeze," "the new broom," or whatever the euphemism. *Therefore, bureaucratic organizations cannot be changed from the top.*

It is difficult for change to come from within, no matter how much internal agitation, because of the division of tasks and the interlocking peer relationships at the same level. Peers live with the motto, "Live and let live." None has the authority to change the work of others. Each runs the risk of sanctions by his peers if he tries to do so. Relationships with superiors are of a reporting kind, and downward control is limited by tradition, policy, regulations, and similar constraints. Besides, there is no official permission to effect change. People are hired to do jobs, not to change the organization. If the organization is inefficient, it is someone else's job to correct it. Employees have neither the authority nor the responsibility and would be extruded from the system if they tried. *Therefore, bureaucratic organizations cannot be changed from the inside.*

It is equally difficult to change organizations from the outside. Critics may flay the organization, commissions investigate it, and consultants ply it with recommendations—to little avail. While the outsiders' criticisms and recommendations may make the insiders feel uncomfortable, even inadequate, these must be implemented by the top or by those within the bureaucracy. As we have seen, neither can effect significant adaptive change. *Therefore, bureaucratic organizations cannot be changed from the outside.*

If bureaucracies cannot be changed by the top, by the inside, or by the outside, the only condition under which they can be changed is when there is a concatenation of all three forces: pressures from the top, the inside, and the outside.

The fortunate set of circumstances, delineated below, precipitated the change effort, the principles of which I shall now discuss.

HISTORICAL BACKGROUND

External Forces

For more than two decades, the Department of State had been the target of criticism because of its failure to change its thinking and practices. This criticism further eroded the self-confidence of a department whose morale had already been severely shaken by the vicious attacks of the McCarthy era. The department, particularly its Foreign Service component, resisted all efforts intended to provide it with the management skills and practices required to carry out the heavy new responsibilities that the rapid expansion of its overseas activities had imposed on it. The resulting loss of leadership in the management of foreign affairs created a power vacuum that was quickly filled by other persons and agencies, which further undermined the department's morale. By the end of the 1960s, there was increasing talk in the Congress of a major reorganization of the foreign affairs agencies which could well have led to the disappearance of the Department of State and the Foreign Service as presently known.

Proposals for the reform of the State Department and its international career component, the Foreign Service, from the 1940s to the 1960s, repeated the same themes. These concerned the traditional aversion of the Foreign Service—staffed largely by academic-intellectual "diplomat" types—toward the management of operational programs as contrasted with the making of policy and related questions of organization, practices, and policies.

Pressures from the Top

Secretaries Cordell Hull and John Foster Dulles believed strongly that the department should be a policy rather than an operating agency. The specialized intelligence, economic, and information activities in which the United States had become involved during World War II were placed under temporary agencies. This view was endorsed by the Hoover commission in 1949. Under President Kennedy, the opposing view prevailed. Unfortunately, the department did not immediately respond to this unprecedented grant of authority by developing the staff capability and management techniques necessary to exercise it effectively. Efforts to evolve managerial practices and programs in response to this change ultimately failed because of too little involvement by the rank and file of the Foreign Service Officer Corps in the development of the program. These programs were conceived at the top, and management tried to impose them from the top.

However, following the report of the Wriston committee in 1954, the Foreign Service revised the conception of its officers from generalists to specialists. There were other studies, other reports, but little significant change.

Internal Forces

Pressures from the outside and from the top failed to produce significant reform. However, there began to be a growing conviction among Foreign Service officers themselves that reform was needed. A survey of the diplomatic profession carried out privately among Foreign Service officers in 1966 showed that a majority of the nearly 600 Foreign Service officers who answered the questionnaires looked favorably on the development of new foreign affairs tools and programs; on the enlargement of the Foreign Service Officer Corps by recruiting people skilled in functions other than traditional diplomacy; on a strong management role for the ambassador; and on assignment of responsibility to the State Department for directing the overseas operations of all agencies.

The department undertook sensitivity training for a number of its senior officers.[2] But this effort was subsequently halted. Chris Argyris prepared a study paper highly critical of the department's rigidity.[3] Subsequently, the American Foreign Service Association (a professional organization of Foreign Service officers) became an active

---

[2] Alfred J. Marrow, "Managerial Revolution in the State Department," *Personnel*, 43:6 (November–December 1966), pp. 8–18.

[3] Chris Argyris, *Some Causes of Organizational Ineffectiveness Within the Department of State*, Occasional Papers Number 2, Center for International Systems Research, Department of State Publication 8180, January 1967.

force for reform, particularly the adoption of modern managerial practices.

In 1969 the State Department came under new leadership, consisting of Secretary William Rogers and Under Secretary Elliott Richardson, and later joined by a new deputy under secretary for administration, William Macomber. They had a charge from the President to do something about the State Department. They had few alternatives: They could employ still another blue ribbon panel or a management consulting firm, or try once again to reinstill vitality by fiat. Since these techniques had failed, a new approach was required. A group of young Foreign Service officers called upon two organizational psychologists, Dr. Alfred Marrow and me (with whom the department had had long previous relationships), to meet for a one-day management seminar to discuss alternative reform possibilities. Richardson and Macomber, both experienced administrators, together with their personal staffs, met for a day in November 1969 with the two organizational psychologists. Both psychologists spoke of the need to "open up" the department, to create a problem-solving atmosphere where energies could be devoted to creative adaptation rather than to defensive conformity. I felt that the crucial need was to create avenues through which the ego-ideal motivation of people in the department could quickly be turned into creative action. I suggested that a series of task forces be established, made up of department personnel across all levels, to study the department's problems simultaneously and make recommendations for change. The logic of this recommendation was that since the top could not adequately change internal arrangements, these had to be acted on by those who were closest to them, who were affected by them, and who could see their limitations. My underlying assumption was that those on the inside knew their problems and probable solutions better than anyone else. Further, when significant numbers of people in the department were involved in self-criticism and adaptive change, a new attitude would be developed about the bureaucracy: namely, that it was a structure amenable to change by those who worked in it in order to serve its own and their needs better. The comments of the two organizational psychologists struck a responsive chord, because it was during this period that discussions were going on among the leaders of the department concerning the possibility of requesting the professionals to examine their own bureaucracy.

Under the direct leadership of Macomber, the department undertook to reform itself from within, an activity virtually without precedent in large organizations. Macomber.asked his principal assistants for a comprehensive list of improvements to be made. In a major speech in January 1970, he summarized several hundred ideas as a series of issues. In that speech he also advocated greater creativity, freedom, openness, and innovation within the department.

Task Force Program

Now all three conditions for change were present: pressure from the outside, pressure from the top, and pressure from the inside. Macomber's speech constituted permission to the department's staff to become involved in the change process.

Following his speech, Macomber appointed 13 task forces to address themselves to that many topics: career management and assignment policies under functional specialization; performance appraisal and promotion policies; personnel requirements and resources; personnel training for the Department of State; personnel prerequisites: nonsalary compensations and allowances; recruitment and employment; stimulation of creativity; role of the country director; openness in the foreign affairs community; reorganization of the Foreign Service Institute; roles and functions of diplomatic missions; management evaluation system; management tools.

It was clearly understood that this was an effort by the Foreign Service and not by the management of the department. The task force chairmen were chosen from the ablest and most experienced officers of the department. They included four ambassadors or former ambassadors, five deputy assistant secretaries and three office directors. Each task force was composed of about 20 members drawn from all levels of the Foreign Service, from the most junior to the most senior, with some admixture of officers from the United States Information Agency and the Agency for International Development. Members were chosen from nominations made by the American Foreign Service Association, from candidates suggested by various Foreign Service officers, and from among volunteers. The task force members were instructed that they were not to represent the official views of the offices to which they were currently assigned but were to serve as officers of the department contributing their own views and thoughts to the task force process.

Each task force was given complete freedom to conduct its work as it saw fit and to make whatever recommendations it chose. It was most important to establish the concept of freedom to examine any problem, inasmuch as the practices of the task forces ideally would serve as models for continuing self-correction efforts. Besides, there were, justifiably, many skeptics.

Following the appointment of the task forces, I met with the 13 chairmen who now constituted a steering group. Despite the publicly stated permission from Macomber to undertake forthright and critical study, a number of the chairmen hesitated. In part, they were reflecting the skeptical attitude of many of the task force members. Did Macomber really want an objective analysis? Or was this just another "reform from the top" under a different guise? On various occasions I and members of Macomber's staff reassured the skeptics and cynics that the effort was a serious one, and that there was a need to legitimize dissent and turn it to constructive ends. I also briefed the chairmen on task force techniques (interview, observation, questionnaire, group discussion), answered questions about procedures, and assured them of continued administrative and consultative support. The assurance carried some weight because of my previous relationship and contact with the department, which they could check out for themselves.

Complementing the steering group of chairmen, there was another group developed especially for those task forces dealing with management problems. The executive secretaries of task forces 7–13 were drawn from the management staff of the department. These seven met weekly to exchange progress reports and discuss mutual problems. These meetings eliminated potential overlap and kept each abreast of the work of the others. These two linkages at the chairman and executive secretary level were crucial to the maintenance of a smooth task force operational process.

The task forces, involving more than 250 officers, met on an average of once a week, mostly during extended lunch periods or in the evenings. The decision to proceed on a part-time basis was deliberate: Management felt that only in this way could it obtain the support of the best talent in the department and the Foreign Service. Thus the work of task force members was in addition to their regular duties. After their initial discussions, most of the task forces divided themselves into subgroups, each responsible for a different aspect of their general topic. The task forces consulted a number of senior department officials and ambassadors, both past and present, interviewed dozens of Foreign Service officers and sent questionnaires to hundreds more, conducted open meetings in order to hear the views of department personnel, and met with consultants outside the department. The time during which their work was done constituted a period of great ferment, in that individual task force members discussed their problems and views with their colleagues, thereby stimulating vigorous debate about the various issues to be considered. The task force effort became the single most discussed subject in the halls of the Department of State. The intensity of the task forces' effort is reflected by the fact that they were able to complete their work in about five months.

As the task forces moved toward the consolidation of their findings, the chairmen met again with me, this time to discuss the feedback process. Rather than turn the reports in to Macomber, I suggested that each chairman present his task force draft report orally to him and subsequently to the secretary and the under secretary, the assistant secretaries and other levels of the department. By presenting their draft reports to all levels of the department, they could encounter, entertain, and reflect the inevitable hostility that would accompany the first feedback. My reasoning was that when personnel at the various levels had the opportunity to see the drafts, criticize them, and respond to their recommendations, after having been heard and having had an influence on the outcome, they would be more inclined to accept the conclusions and facilitate the implementation.

The chairmen were initially reluctant to undertake these briefings. However, both Macomber and I were adamant about the necessity for such dialogues. Therefore, extensive discussions were scheduled with personnel at all levels of management, starting with the secretary and the under secretary, both of whom devoted several hours to listening to the conclusions of the various task forces. Intensive consultations were also undertaken with assistant secretaries and their staffs, and special meetings were held for members of the department's "Open Forum," a group of the more junior officers.

Subsequently, the task force draft reports were circulated to various components of the department and to embassies abroad. Great stress was placed on the fact that these reports were still in the draft stage, since it was important to assure people that their comments would be taken into consideration before the reports were put in final form.

After employees in the department were given adequate time to review the draft reports, another series of meetings was held. One set of meetings was for assistant secretaries and their deputies, another for mid-management personnel, and a third for the rank and file. In all these meetings, the chairmen of the task forces or one of the task force members answered questions or defended the task forces' views. This was an important aspect of the whole philosophy of the reform program. Since the reports were written by members of the department and the Foreign Service, it was vital for the members of the task forces to be included in the dialogue with their colleagues who were involved. Had a member of management, as contrasted with the Foreign Service, been placed in the position of defending the reports, the whole philosophical basis for the reform program would have been destroyed. Furthermore, State Department administrators themselves felt that the staff, which would be responsible for the implementation of the program, should not be burdened by the criticism that employees might make of the reports themselves.

The comments that arose from these consultations were carefully reviewed, and many were incorporated by the task forces before the reports were submitted in final form. There was general support on the part of both domestic employees and overseas personnel for the conclusions reached by the task forces.

The task forces had begun their work in February 1970. By the end of June they had issued their first drafts. Then a period of three months elapsed while the drafts were circulated and comments were incorporated into the final report. By the end of September, almost all the reports had been submitted in final form and were ready to be compiled into one for submission to the Secretary of State. It had been recognized early in the process that inconsistencies would arise and that the 13 reports would have to be integrated into the general

framework of a summary report. Because of earlier coordinating
efforts already discussed, although some inconsistencies were
present, there were not nearly as many nor were they as difficult to
reconcile as had been originally anticipated. On the contrary, management was pleased by the explicit and implicit repetition of certain
central themes.

The drafting of the summary report was assigned to a new special
assistant to Macomber, Petrow, who had also been the chairman of
one of the task forces. By the end of November, the summary had
been written and the total report was ready for submission to the
Secretary of State. Taken as a whole, the 13 reports constituted a formidable document, some 600 pages in length with about 500 individual recommendations.[4] The Secretary of State, who had maintained
an active interest in the program during this whole process, was thoroughly briefed by the 13 task force chairmen. He was able, therefore,
upon receipt of the reports to approve them in principle and to direct Macomber to begin immediately an active implementation process.

This process consisted of assigning each recommendation to one of
five categories. The first category included those recommendations
that had been approved for immediate implementation. The second
and third categories consisted of recommendations that were to be
implemented within 90 or 180 days, respectively. The fourth category included recommendations that required further study and
about which the time of decision was indefinite. The fifth category,
which was quite small, consisted of recommendations that had been
disapproved.

At the time this chapter was written it was too early to reach any
firm conclusions about the long-term efficacy of this internal reform
program. However, even at that early stage, there were a number of
findings.

(1) It is not impossible for members of an organization to take a hard,
    critical, and objective look at themselves. The correlation between
    the criticisms made by the task forces and the comments made by

---

[4] *Diplomacy for the 70's*, Department and Foreign Service Series 143, Department
of State Publication 8551, December 1970.

outsiders about the Department of State during the 1960s was extremely high. If anything, the task forces were probably harder on the department and its employees than more objective observers might have been.

(2) The reputation of certain officers among their peers and subordinates changed when their colleagues discovered that these officers would concur in certain "progressive" conclusions reached by the task forces of which they were members.

(3) The reform program proved that an organization could accept criticisms from its members without incurring negative consequences. It demonstrated also that officers could speak up without running the risk of penalties.

(4) Almost everyone involved agreed that the self-education process of task force members was beneficial in itself. Many misconceptions about the department's way of doing business evaporated as the task forces went through the process of learning how things were being done, not only in the department but in other parts of the government and in American business. The skepticism of many members of the task forces at the beginning of the process disappeared as they developed their reports. Many continued to urge more rapid implementation of the recommendations.

(5) The reform program proved that management can evoke a large range of excellent ideas from all parts of an organization. Given an opportunity, most people will respond to challenges presented to them and will, in a free and democratic atmosphere, be creative and responsible.

In his report on the first 90-day implementation progress, Macomber indicated that the department had launched its first major new personnel program since 1954, the Foreign Affairs Specialist Corps, to attract more specialists and to incorporate them within a single personnel system; that personnel authority had been centralized and major changes had been made in its practices; that recruitment practices had been expanded to include a wider range of institutions and specialties; that performance review and evaluation processes were being changed to give more recognition to creativity and proficiency in achieving specific objectives and to discourage conformity; that the department was well along in the development of a modern organizational concept that will support the principal officers of the department in carrying out an integrated process of planning, decision making, implementing, and relating resources to policy and program evaluation, both inside the department and outside in relationship to other agencies; that a management evaluation group had been created to evaluate the effectiveness of United States foreign policies and programs; that respective bureaus within the department were developing processes to support their managerial responsibilities; and that 200 of the 489 approved task force recommendations had been implemented. All this, he said, was really only a start toward setting in motion a process of change.

The import of the simultaneous task force method lies, significantly, in the last sentence: that it set in motion a continuous process of self-correction; that it created an atmosphere in which people within the system were expected to work on their own organizational problems; that it legitimized the concept of openness in intraorganizational relationship; and that it created the conditions for managerial creativity. Now, of course, the question is, "Can the process work on a continuing basis?"

The task forces recommended some devices to insure that it would. They urged that the top management in the department make a concerted effort to loosen the chain of command through greater use of ad hoc task forces, staffed by personnel of all ranks, to deal with specific problems and issues, not only in missions abroad, as noted earlier, but in the department as well. They argued that officers working in the informal, unstructured setting of a task force, freed from constraints of rank, would express themselves with greater independence and originality. They also recommended that, in the formal presentation of policy recommendations to senior levels, officers from subordinate echelons be permitted to be present and be encouraged to state their views, even if different from those of their immediate superiors. The task forces also made several recommendations for democratizing United States missions abroad in the belief that the hierarchic structure that has grown up around the traditional, somewhat authoritarian concept of the role of the ambassador, is increasingly irrelevant to the requirements of the modern diplomat-manager.

Of course, a crucial issue in any organization is leadership. That issue cannot be overcome merely by building new managerial structures or introducing new processes. A fundamental reorientation to their work and function will be required of Foreign Service officers who must now see themselves, not as diplomats, but as manager-diplomats. New managerial procedures will be useless if the department's officers remain unconvinced that management of resources should be the department's role, or if they fail to assert personal leadership in the interagency forums in which this role is played. Nor will it accomplish anything to open up channels for the communication of new ideas if officers are inhibited by bureaucratic caution from using these channels. New methods for promoting openness will not succeed if officers are unable to overcome their traditional resistance to ideas from the outside. Such problems may well require other forms of group process experiences, which Dr. Marrow eloquently advocated.

The leadership of the department is committed to the implementation of the program as developed by the task forces. There is no longer any doubt that the great preponderance of the recommendations will be instituted. The leadership of the department is not only encouraging the organization to develop more adaptive attitudes but also, in collaboration with the Foreign Service Association, is pushing the department in the direction of greater flexibility. Pressure from the top and the inside, together with continued criticism from the outside, remain. Now that it has mechanisms for constructive change, continued evolution should follow.

CONCLUSION

Despite outstanding achievements by individual officers, the Department of State as an organization has been disappointing, to itself, to the public, and to successive Presidents, in its putative role of directing and coordinating both the formulation and execution of foreign policy. The principal cause of this disappointing performance has been its encrusted bureaucratic structure and its weakness in management capability. The traditional reliance of the Foreign Service officer on experience and intuition is no longer enough. He must now be a diplomat-manager, backed by an organization based on modern management principles, since the central task of foreign policy coordination is allocation of resources among competing interests—a key management function. In the past, the department and Foreign Service officers were loath to accept this view. Like all major bureaucracies, the department has been guilty of excessive caution and a tendency to defend established policies and programs beyond their point of diminishing returns.

Neither official flaying, public criticism, nor internal grumbling over a period of decades has been sufficient to change this bureaucracy. Bureaucratic structures cannot respond to any of these forces, and simple reorganization merely creates another bureaucratic form. When three forces were present simultaneously—external discontent, leadership discontent, and internal discontent—and a mechanism was established for continuous reformation of structure from within, the first step was taken in revitalizing the organization and bringing it face to face with its realities. That mechanism (in this case multiple, simultaneous task forces) must be appropriate for the developmental stage of the organization, taking into account the degree of support it requires from the consultant, its level of competence and skill to effect changes, and its capacity for mastering its own problems. In addition it must allow for the ego ideal of the organization to serve as a motivating and unifying force and enhance the self-images of organization members. Thus, the psychological man conception is extended to the organization. And such a method would seem to be applicable to many other types of organizations.

CHAPTER 10

Organizational Development
Versus Organizational Diagnosis

IF THESE ISSUES OF INDIVIDUAL and organizational adaptation are
valid, then it becomes imperative to have sufficient understanding of
both individuals and organizations to bring about the effective interaction of both for their mutual benefit. In this chapter, I want to suggest caution about the disproportionate emphasis on one or the
other, particularly, given the contemporary emphasis on organizational development, on that preoccupation with organizational
change which does not take into account psychological man conceptions. I think it is important to alert managers and executives to
the hazards and risks of disproportionate emphasis so that they may
make their choices of consultants and processes more wisely. It is not
my intention here to condemn, but to balance. Just as a physician
may treat a physical pain with medication, without raising questions
about psychological issues which may have precipitated it, similarly
many people may become involved in treating an organizational pain
on the basis of interventions that do not adequately take into account
the psychology of the individuals involved or the comprehensive conception of what the organization is all about. The manager or the executive has the ultimate responsibility for what happens to him and
his organization. He cannot leave that to specialists who, after all, by
definition are just that—experts in one area.

In recent years there has been considerable concern with organizational change and organizational development. Much of this con-

cern has stemmed from the group dynamics movement, and those who have practiced organizational development have been largely social psychologists, sociologists, and others in a variety of disciplines who have applied variations of group dynamics techniques. A limited number of clinical psychologists have also been involved in this new direction.

Like nondirective counseling, organization development practices concentrate largely on having people talk to each other about their mutual working interests and problems; on working together on the resolution of common problems; and on having people weigh, out loud and with each other, their organizational aspirations and goals. These efforts are largely devoid of systematic theory. They are often problem-specific and frequently intuitive. It is presumed by their practitioners that the same general methods will apply to all organizations.

The field of organizational development is presently in a fluid state, marked primarily by ad hoc problem-solving efforts and by a heavy emphasis on expedient techniques, ranging from games to confrontation. Frequently the rationale behind these techniques is poorly thought through, and the fact that the techniques sometimes precipitate untoward consequences is either unrecognized or denied by many who claim to be experts in organizational development. However, as any skilled clinician knows, not all patients will prosper equally well with the same therapy, and there are severe limitations to that kind of intervention that merely enables people to clarify their conscious feelings and to work on problems consciously perceived. For dealing with more complex problems at deeper levels, the clinician—whether psychologist or psychiatrist—requires a comprehensive theory of personality and a range of interventions from which to choose techniques flexibly as the therapy progresses.

Little of what is presently called organizational development involves anything like formal diagnosis. For example, while it is traditional for a responsible clinical psychologist to evaluate his client or patient both from the point of view of that person's problems and the capacity he has for dealing with them—and most psychologists would find it irresponsible to work with clients or patients without formulating an understanding of what they are dealing with—such processes are not within the purview of most people involved in organizational development. It is my contention that a professional cannot act responsibly in consultation, whether individual or organizational, unless he maintains a scientific point of view about what he does. To me, this means that he must formulate a diagnosis, which is essentially a working hypothesis about what he is dealing with. Then he must formulate methods—whether they be treatment, intervention, training experiences, or other devices—that will be effective tests of the hypothesis he proposes or that will compel him to revise his hypothesis and change his methods accordingly.

A diagnosis, whether of an individual or an organization, requires a comprehensive examination of the client's system. That examination of the individual who is a client will frequently involve measures of intelligence and intellective or cognitive functions and modes of assessing psychological defenses and coping mechanisms, managing emotions, and pinpointing focal conflicts. A thorough examination will also require understanding personal history as the context for character formation and styles of adaptation. The examination will frequently involve psychological testing and often consultation with a neurologist, pediatrician, or psychiatrist. Indeed, some psychologists specialize in diagnosis alone, a process so helpful that in many of the best kinds of psychological and psychiatric clinics such diagnostic formulations guide the therapy regardless of who conducts it. Thus, a comprehensive examination, leading to a sensitive and sophisticated diagnostic statement, becomes the basis for predicting the best kind of therapeutic process, its likely course and outcome, and possible danger points. That process also permits the professional to review what goes on in his relationship with his client, to modify his behavior and activity in keeping with changes in his diagnostic hypotheses, and, ultimately, to compare his examinational findings at different points in time to measure progress.

It is quite unfortunate that this process seems not to be an intrinsic part of contemporary organizational development, but there are a number of reasons why. There is no systematic body of professional knowledge about organizational development. Most books on the subject are fragmentary, made up of unintegrated papers. Most techniques are ad hoc, with limited rationale. Many, if not most, people who work with organizational development have had limited training, some having no more than attended sensitivity training groups or, at best, having had only a brief internship in conducting sensitivity training. Most have had no training in depth to understand the dynamics of individual personality (even those who have degrees in social psychology or sociology), let alone any sophisticated understanding of group processes. Many lean heavily on psychological cliches like "self-actualization" or similar slogans derived from rubrics used in psychological research without refining these rubrics into syndromes or formulations that create the conditions for intervention. Finally, much organizational development seems to hinge on one device, *namely*, confrontation, which, when it is the single technique for all problems, necessarily becomes merely a gimmick. With respect to organizational development, we are at that point in time comparable to the use of leeches in medicine. Just as they served the purpose of drawing bad blood, so the single technique in organizational development seems to be justified in terms of serving the purpose of drawing out bad feelings or emotions.

FAILURE TO DIAGNOSE AND THE CONSEQUENCES

This state of affairs inevitably leads to certain kinds of failures, disillusionments, destructive consequences, and other negative outcomes that ultimately cause the public—in this case, the companies or other institutions—to withdraw, as many have, from sensitivity training and encounter techniques. Following are some case examples where the failure to diagnose led to untoward consequences.

A rigid, authoritarian company president, who built his organization into international prominence, was disappointed by the fact that he could not seem to retain a corps of young managers who had top management executive potential. While he hired many, they left after two or three years with the organization, usually moving up into higher level roles in other companies. He himself attributed this loss to an inadequate management development program and sought the help of a social scientist well versed in the concept of confrontation. Certain that the problem was the president himself, and equally certain that he would profit by attack from his subordinates, the social scientist arranged an organizational development program whose first steps included just that kind of confrontation. In the course of the experience, the president became livid with frustrated rage, angry that his paternalism was unappreciated, and abandoned his efforts to develop the company further. In impulsive anger, he sold it, a fact that ultimately cost him dearly and enmeshed his management in the adaptive problems of a merger which made his company merely an appendage of a larger organization.

A major division of a large corporation undertook, with the help of a prominent and responsible consultant, an organizational development program intended to "open things up" in order to foster group cooperation. Shortly after this developmental effort, the division head was removed from his position because it was discovered that he had manipulated and exploited his subordinates, that he had sponsored orgies at sales meetings in violation of company ethics, and that he had, in various other psychopathic ways, acted irresponsibly and manipulatively. The consultant, however well qualified in working with groups, knew nothing about individual psychology and, as a result, his efforts to "open people up" served only to make people potentially more vulnerable to exploitation. Under such circumstances that group of managers would have been much better off to have learned ways of becoming more highly guarded and protected.

A company president, in an effort to solve a problem of long-standing conflict between him and two vice presidents reporting to him (whom he could not discharge), sought occasional professional advice on how to deal with this problem. The severely intense nature of the conflict reflected not only chronic irritation but certain obvious neurotic problems that required individual therapy for two of the three men involved. Both disdained such help. One of the vice presidents, impressed with the work of a trainer involved in team building in a division, persuaded the president to use the trainer to help the three of them resolve their conflict. The president agreed. The trainer's mode of working was to attack and pry loose the feelings of hostility, which he then required to be exhibited publicly. This mode of attack, like evangelistic fervor of old, served the purpose of making the president confess his "guilt" and his inadequacies, which the trainer required to be done not only in the presence of the two vice presidents but, subsequently, in the presence of the whole group of managers who reported to them. The president became increasingly depressed and was referred for psychiatric consultation. Meanwhile, the remaining managerial group, now subject to psychologizing attack from the president and vice presidents, as well as from the trainer (who made it known to all that he was making the decisions about managers' careers), awaited apprehensively their turn to be exposed. Furthermore, as the president became increasingly depressed, the story started circulating in managerial ranks that the vice president who brought the trainer in was using him to destroy the president. When the trainer was confronted by others about the destructive effect on the president of what he was doing, he denied that he needed to have knowledge about such effects, saying that he was only "training" people and did not claim to be a psychologist (though he was a member of The American Psychological Association) or a psychiatrist.

A major consulting organization undertook to advise on the drastic reorganization of a client firm. The consequence of this drastic reorganization was that many people who had previously held power were successfully emasculated of their power although they retained their positions. The firm traditionally had insisted on and rewarded compliance so these men did not openly complain, but there was widespread depression and anger among them for which the consulting firm assumed no responsibility. In fact, it is doubtful whether their developmental efforts included any recognition of the psychological consequences of what they did.

As part of a developmental effort in a company, thought to be a wise course to "open people up," a trainer undertook encounter experiences that involved having the executives touch each other and engage in activities that brought them physically closer to each other. Two executives, whose latent homosexual impulses (unconscious and well controlled) could not tolerate such closeness, had psychotic breaks, and had to be hospitalized.

A trainer undertook a two-day intensive session with a group of managers in a company and required them to tell each other what problems they had with other managers and what they thought of each other's on-the-job behavior. This was, in many respects, a cathartic session, which discharged much hostility, presumably in preparation for cooperative work. However, when the management in the organization failed to follow up and, indeed, began to see the now "opened up" group as a threat to its power and tried to disband it as an effective group, the participants became disillusioned and angry and now pulled farther away from each other. Having expressed their hostility to each other for the purpose of common good, they now had to live with their hostile expressions when there was no longer a common good. They began to avoid each other and to feel guilty for their expressions as they awaited retaliation from those whom they had criticized.

The cases just cited are examples of the destructive consequences of organizational consultation without diagnosis. I could offer many more examples, but these will suffice.

FORMAL DIAGNOSTIC PROCESS

In order for a consultant to avoid these kinds of consequences, he must have a systematic knowledge of individual motivation, as well as organizational and small group theory, and be able to evolve modes of intervention based on diagnoses that include that multiple level understanding. Now, by way of contrast, I will illustrate, with several cases, what I think a formal diagnostic process should provide.

As discussed in Chapter 9, the State Department had been subject to widespread criticism, several outside commissions, sensitivity training, and a variety of other interventions, to little or no avail. The problems of its bureaucracy remained and still had to be dealt with. Diagnosis of that system indicated that an organizational structure was unlikely to be changed by pressure from the outside alone, pressure from the inside alone, or pressure from leadership alone. It could not be altered significantly by sensitivity training methods alone, as had already been demonstrated, or by leadership. If the basic problems were structural, that is, bureaucratic, then change could occur only by altering the whole structure and by evolving mechanisms for keeping it open. This conception led to the establishment of 13 task forces (including about 20 people each) operating simultaneously. Thus, some 250 people were turned loose in a self-critical appraisal of their own structure. They produced from this a 600-page volume and have since had a series of follow-up outcome statements on their recommendations. There was minimal work by the consultant, which consisted largely in his instructing the task force leaders, supporting organizational leadership, and helping the task force leaders and the organizational leadership anticipate the kinds of hostility they were going to encounter.

A president with a good managerial history was brought in to head a scientific company whose key men neither understood nor wanted to be subject to professional management. When they threatened to resign, and some did, urgent consultation was requested. Diagnosis of this situation took into account organizational history and scientific values, desertion by the company's founders, exploitation by a previous president, cohesion of the in-group, and the need to retain adaptive profitability. On the basis of a comprehensive assessment, it was decided to hear the men out in individual interviews, then summarize those interviews and present them simultaneously to the interviewees and the president. This procedure produced problems and issues to be dealt with, without subjecting the group to the possible exploitation of the president, whom they feared, and without running the risk of their destroying him under confrontation attack. The consultant became, in effect, an intermediary. On the one hand, his job was to help the president understand the nature of the complaints and the kinds of people he was dealing with as well as certain basic psychological principles. On the other hand, his task was to help the group recognize its need for a professional manager and to offer these men more constructive ways of giving the president support and guidance. After the initial contacts of three, three-day sessions, the consultant maintained a distance from the group so that he would not be seen as "running the company." Many of the key managers individually took part in executive seminars to learn more about the psychology of management, and the consultant was available to all of them as individuals by phone or personal contact. This enabled the president and his key figures to develop a working relationship in which all could count on the distant but supportive influence of the consultant and the new and consistent pattern of leadership the president established.

Once general comfort was attained in these relationships and the men could come to trust the president (in part because the consultant drew off some of their hostility toward him), they decided that it would be wise to get together as a group at monthly intervals in order to open up avenues of communication, which they knew needed opening but which would have been destructively explosive had they been opened before. The group continues to function effectively together, now more closely than ever. However, this process of carefully differentiated steps extended over a three-year period.

Following the devastating effect of the reorganization of a company (mentioned in the fourth case in the previous discussion) and a subsequent year of turmoil, a consultant was asked to undo the situation. Initial interviews with the executives indicated the severity of the depression each was experiencing and provided information on the turmoil in the rest of the organization. Building upon a clinical understanding of depression following the experience of loss, an appreciation of the sense of responsibility the managers in the organization felt, the sensitivity of the new leadership, and important changes in external forces which the organization now confronted, the consultant recommended that the 100 top management people be brought together for a meeting to last several days. During this meeting, on the consultant's recommendation, the chief executive officer presented the history of the organization, its achievements, its present state, and its future potential, and indicated clearly what was happening in the outside environment and what drastic changes had to be made. This was followed by an opportunity for the 100 men, in small groups, to discuss and analyze what they had heard and to mourn the loss as well as to confront reality. While regretting the past, they could begin to see clearly what the future held and what kinds of adaptive efforts might have to be made.

They were then reconvened to hear presentations about future trends in their field, as well as in society at large, and to set in context what they were up against. They then had the opportunity to discuss and digest their impressions and to see how such forces related to them. On the basis of those small-group discussions, they established priorities for action, coalesced them in large plenary sessions, and evolved a charter for their functional operations. Thus, they began to turn their aggressions outward on real problems, which they faced together, while working through their sense of loss and depression.

The president of a small corporation, wanted to develop an adaptive executive team on the one hand but, on the other, had the paranoid feeling that such a group would steal his business from him. I say paranoid because that was an important component of his personality. The consultant's diagnosis was that open confrontation would only reinforce his paranoid feelings and frighten him into withdrawing from his people further. Instead, the consultant chose to work directly with the president for a time, helping him spell out his fears and testing his suspicions of the consultant in a one-to-one relationship. Once that relationship could contain the suspicious hostility of the president, the consultant met with the vice presidents who reported to the president, got their view of the working relationship, and translated that for the president in ways that enabled him to understand the effects of his behavior without feeling attacked. Subsequently, the vice presidents and president were brought together to talk about these issues, with the consultant as a medium for trust and control. With that kind of process in motion, the consultant began to work with the 20 men who were the third echelon, taking them as a group through their working relationships and their managerial skills, now less afraid that they might be attacked by a suspicious, impulsive president for asserting their independence.

I cite these examples, not to illustrate in detail a diagnostic process, but to indicate that one was in motion which required different interventions for different organizations and with different people under varying circumstances. Whether the diagnoses made were the correct ones is not the point. Inasmuch as they were made consciously, they could exist as testable hypotheses, always subject to change. The consultant could then make interventions of choice. In effect, he exercised control over what was happening, testing his choices rather than assuming that one method worked equally well in all circumstances.

DEALING WITH PSYCHOLOGICAL POLLUTION

There is a devastating trend of psychological pollution in contemporary organizational circles. Destructive influences arise out of merger, reorganization, individual and organizational obsolescence, and change. These forces will continue for the foreseeable future. That kind of pollution can be dealt with through the medium of organizational intervention, providing the consultant has sufficient understanding of diagnostic and therapeutic conceptions to discern the phenomena he is dealing with and to be able to act on them. We cannot afford the continued blundering by untrained people, which is destructive to organizations and to individuals, but we do have resources to deal with the problems.

First, executives can draw more heavily on clinically trained personnel. The clinical psychologist and psychiatrist, trained as they are in individual diagnosis and therapy, have a basic frame of reference for looking at organizational problems in the same way. Many are already working with families as systems. If encouraged to do so, many can extend their knowledge and, subsequently, their efforts to include organizations as systems. Such work requires a formal diagnostic process built on clinical skills but expanded to view the organization as the client system and to include group and organizational processes.

Clinicians can extend their diagnostic frame of reference, as I have recently done,[1] by evolving a five-step procedure. This procedure

---

[1] Harry Levinson, *Organizational Diagnosis* (Cambridge, Mass.: Harvard University Press, 1972).

should include: (1) a detailed organizational history that will delineate both the forces impinging on the organization over time and its characteristic adaptive pattern and its modes for coping with crisis; (2) a description of the organization that would include its organizational structure, physical facilities, people, finances, practices and procedures, policies, values, technology, and context in which the organization operates; (3) an interpretation of observations, interviews, questionnaires, and other information about the organization's characteristic ways of receiving, processing, and acting upon information, as well as the personality characteristics of the dominant organizational figures and the style of organizational personality; (4) a summary and interpretation of all these findings with a diagnostic formulation; (5) a feedback report to the organization to establish a basis for organizational action toward solving its problems.

Such a process is extended from and based on the clinical case study method. It views the organization as an open system with a range of semiautonomous interacting subsystems. Both the subsystems and the organization as a total system can be evaluated in terms of how effectively they adapt to the environments in which they operate, where organizational and subsystem strengths and weaknesses lie, and what kinds of steps can be delineated to utilize the assets to cope with the weaknesses. In undertaking this kind of organizational diagnostic process, the clinician must give careful attention to the psychology of the individual people involved and to the collective psychology of groups, since many people working in the same organization share common elements of personality.

Second, the nonclinician familiar with group and organizational processes but unfamiliar with personality theory and clinical diagnostic practice can expand his learning to include both. There are clinical training resources in most large communities. There are also many individual clinicians who can serve as training consultants for people who need that kind of preparation.

The ultimate practice of organizational development might better be called "applied clinical sociology." The executive who is to make use of such techniques should therefore be certain his consultant is well trained in both dimensions—clinical and organizational. In practice, such a consultant usually gives careful attention to leadership and continued work with the leadership. His feedback of his diagnosis to the client system or his guidance of an organizational team to formulate a diagnostic statement becomes the basis for formulating common action. He deals with both positive and negative unrealistic expectations of himself. In the last analysis, such a consultation is the management of a relationship between the consultant and the organizational system—thus a problem of clinical management for therapeutic purposes.

The need for such a diagnostic process is imperative because of disillusionment not only with organizational development but with many aspects of community change. Despite much talk, community psychology, community psychiatry, and other forms of community organizational development, have not had a significant impact on social systems, such as churches, schools, and similar community agencies. No amount of ad hoc expedience, no amount of talking about "growth," and no amount of depreciating the old as being "in the medical model" will substitute for solid knowledge systematically organized, interpretations based on a comprehensive conceptual system, and diagnostic hypotheses amenable to continuous testing and alterations. Only with a solid clinical base can one come at community and organizational development with a prospect of long-term gain. Inevitably, if he is to have a community impact, the clinician must become an organizational diagnostician, and the organizational development man, a clinician. The wise executive can facilitate that combination of skills by demanding the level of performance that requires it.

CONCLUSION

Many efforts to change organizations are based on economic man or self-actualizing man conceptions. These result in organizational restructuring, manipulation of rewards and punishments, or efforts to foster group interaction and group problem solving. However, based on limited understanding of the individual personality, they frequently produce unintended consequences. These efforts toward change cannot deal with problems where complex psychological issues are at play. Scientifically based interventions require formal diagnostic formulations and choice of methods of change based on such formulations. These require a conception of psychological man to take into account both individual and group processes. The executive who seeks organizational development consultation should require both individual and group levels of sophistication.

CHAPTER 11

Reflections on an Experience

Now I SHOULD LIKE TO MAKE A DRAMATIC SHIFT in emotional focus for both myself and the reader. In doing so, I address the maturational aspect of psychological man for both of us.

The last year of my four-year Business School appointment coincided with my fiftieth year. Both occasions are conducive to reflection. A major part of living is the experience of formulating personal hypotheses, however unconscious, and acting upon them. Reflection is a reexamination of those hypotheses, the assumptions underlying them, and the consequence of having tested them. It is one's mode of creating his own cognitive maps, his way of steering himself in his relationship with people and institutions.

The essence of gratification in living is the continuing feeling of being generative, to use Erikson's term. This is especially true in middle age, a time already burdened with the visible decline of physical resources, the narrowing of interests, and the loss of valued friends. Reflection is an important aspect of generativity in middle age because it is only at that point in time that one begins to have a sufficiently varied range of experience to make abstractions and generalizations from his life that can become his wisdom. It is in the sharing of those abstractions and that wisdom that one facilitates growth in others. It is in that sharing also that one maintains the continuity of his own life experience, for sharing preserves that experience as a tie from the past to the future.

There are three relevant continuities for a professor: his discipline, his students, and his institution. The reader of this volume will have little concern for the continuity of psychology. He should have a more important stake in the institution that prepares the student for leadership in enterprise and generates the knowledge that makes enterprise more effective. He will have an even more important concern for the students upon whom he is likely to call to evolve his own and his organization's continuity, for the reader is likely to be at that point in life when he is concerned with his own generativity.

The end of an experience is, of course, an experience of loss that requires a period of mourning, an expression of one's regret, and one's own restitution efforts. All three are combined for me in these reflections, a brief and personal reaction in the form of a message to the reader about how I have found the students and what the implications may be for him. In so doing, I pass my students on to the reader.

Reflections of a middle-aged college professor are necessarily stimulated by his experience with students. I recall those experiences at the Harvard Business School with great warmth. Students have a capacity for kindling in me that rare delight which comes from mutual teaching and learning. They fascinate me with their early bravado. The Chinese may have invented acupuncture but, in its intellectual form, it lives a lusty existence at the Harvard Business School. Managers and executives may expect similar experience. They will enjoy it or resent it according to the level of their fear.

Of the many executives and students with whom I have worked in one way or another, I find the students in the early days of their first graduate year to be the most challenging. They begin their enforced relationship with poorly masked penetrating probings. Beneath their words are the questions: Who are you? What do you have to teach? Who decided we should learn this? Are you capable of teaching it? Can we trust you? Their testing is undisguised and unrelenting as they examine the potential relationship with their instructor. Their intellectual dissection serves quickly to mark the depth and integrity of the professor as an instrument of professional socialization. This psychological mapping, conducted by vigorous groups some 80 voices strong and magnified in intensity by the centralized focus that an amphitheater classroom provides, operates like a human sonar device. The psychological reverberations re-echo through the classroom; now as the instructor responds to a single student, then as he relates to the group as a whole. The mapping process serves also to provide sometimes painful insight for the instructor himself. He refines his perceptual acuity to the nuances of classroom behavior, or he becomes an intellectual drudge. He can easily fail to develop the former, which results in the latter.

For me the classroom has been an enriching experience. My dismay matches my gratification only when the students become disappointed with "the system." They arrive at that point when they begin to feel that the formal institutional processes inhibit their learning. Then they shift from the zest for learning to the determination to get through under the grinding anger of frustration. They are then sometimes like flowers that on better days seem to stretch for the sun and on cloudy days hang limply as if helpless before the anticipated cold winds. The reader may observe the same behavior among employees in organizations (he will be dismayed if he observes it in his own). He should prepare himself to wage his most vigorous fight against this psychological blight.

In the second year, the students provide another kind of gratification. They invest themselves for long hours with great conscientiousness, particularly in field work in organizations, a task that promises knowledge, insight, and skill. They are willing to invest themselves, to draw from the instructor's experience, to entertain their fears and anxieties about what they are doing, and to mobilize themselves to surmount them. Sometimes I find myself envying the organizations that will employ them, while simultaneously wondering if those prospective employers will be wise enough to keep them challenged and invested, to take advantage of their intense wish to become more effective masters of the problems they confront.

In the second year, the classes are more selective and smaller. Thus the students are closer to being colleagues. The instructor is continuously learning with them and from them as they bring problems from the field and as they test in practice the conceptions he has advanced. They are therefore simultaneously a mode of extending knowledge and conceptions, a group of interdependent allies, extensions of the instructor's conceptual thrust, testers of his assumptions, and unique human beings who critically evaluate in their own daily problem-solving efforts what both he and experience have to offer. Then they adapt this knowledge and incorporate it in the ongoing thrust of their own identities.

Now with a smile, now with a casual remark, now with echoing sarcasm, now with a gentle question, students at both levels keep the instructor humble and honest. They can be tolerant of his shortcomings if he himself is aware of them and tries to compensate for them. Frequently those who are most critical turn out to be those who test most vigorously, for they seek a model on whose solidity they can depend and who will return their hostile probings, not for what manifestly they seem to be, but for the underlying search for affection and guidance that they signify. Managers to whom these young men and women will report will work better with them if these managers understand such behavior. Many, indeed, merit that understanding. Those who seek to understand find that they are personally richer for understanding. Psychological wealth lies immediately in front of every manager. Many find it. When they do, they discover a new and exhilarating dimension to their managerial roles and goals.

CHAPTER 12

Postscript

FLYING IN A JET AIRPLANE AT NIGHT, from 30,000 ft. one can see the lights of distant cities. Here and there groups of lights glow, reflecting the existence of human beings. Knowing cities, one can imagine streets, houses, schools, churches, bridges, rivers, and so on. But, in the darkness, he cannot see them. He cannot see how one street runs into another or where there are traffic problems or gathering places. He can see only more or fewer lights and the proximity of one set of lights to another. In the daylight, things become clearer. One can differentiate buildings, streets, and features of the terrain. He can see the connections among them in the form of roads, streets, paths. He can glimpse beauty, contrast, dimension, vitality. He can determine the respective sites for action, pleasure, recreation, worship, education, and business.

In his businessman role, the executive has all too frequently been in the former position. His task has been to achieve productivity and profitability. To do that, he has been armed with the concepts of industrial engineering and economics. In the last analysis, his yardstick has been return on investment. In earlier days, he needed only to obtain a product and to get it to a marketplace. Subsequently, he had to manufacture that product or process it in some fashion. The years have brought increasing refinement of products and of the marketplace and therefore increasing refinement of techniques of productivity and measuring return on investment. Now, however, the business executive is confronted with a new and broader conception of return on investment—he must take into account people's lives and the environment in which they live and work. Not only must he deal with the broader concept of cost, now including social costs, but he must also deal with changing motivations, which do not respond so well to these historic concepts of industrial engineering and economics. Both of these disciplines regard the person and his motivation either as irrelevant to the effectiveness of the technique or to be dealt with simply on a reward-punishment, jackass, basis.

Faced with these changing circumstances, the executive who sees himself as continuing to be in the dark and therefore unable to discern what exists with sufficient clarity to deal with it, will give up. He will not know how to cope with what is there because he cannot see it or understand it, let alone have an opportunity to act. He who has greater courage may adapt one or another new technique, to be used like dropping a giant flare from the speeding jet—to illuminate one or another dimension of the earth temporarily—which will perhaps provide for him some better notion of where he is, where he's going, and what lies in front of him. But the illumination will be sporadic and inadequate for, by attending only to what is illuminated by those beams, that which he cannot see is left untouched. Therefore, it becomes impractical to depend on fads or techniques. The executive cannot afford to be in a never-ending chase after the latest fad, let alone contend with the consequences of management by fad. What he needs is a comprehensive theory of motivation to help him understand what he is dealing with, what he is likely to be dealing with, and how he might use himself and his resources most effectively. He needs a theory of sufficient complexity that he can become as knowledgeable about motivation as he is about marketing, finance, control, and other business functions. He needs a theory that is subject to the test of his own experience and which will give him understanding rather than clichés. Above all, he needs a theory that will open up for him a range of alternative avenues for action.

Not only does he need to be able to strengthen his own position and to increase his own effectiveness as an executive, both for his own gratification and for the success of the organization, but he will also be increasingly burdened with the task of sustaining his organization. As we have already seen, society can less and less afford to allow business organizations to die. Too much is at stake in the form of social investment, jobs, techniques, guarantees, and so on. Business organizations therefore will have to be managed for their own perpetuation, and the executive, therefore, will more and more be judged on how effectively he does that task. He cannot do it without an adequate understanding of psychological man.

In these pages, I have begun to outline how the executive might better understand contemporary psychological man. I have indicated some of the ways in which a mobile population, no longer able to root itself in small communities or neighborhoods, seeks to identify itself with organizations in order to cope more effectively with its own and organizational problems by acquiring skills and competences and by affiliating itself with organizations for psychological as well as economic reasons. As organizations assume an ever broader and more exacting social role, then those who have affiliated themselves with organizations will be even more alienated and more difficult to manage by reward-punishment conceptions. The executive may be appalled at the complexity of motivation he is being asked to understand and act on. However, as with space flight, what seems to be inordinately difficult and even perhaps impossible eventually becomes commonplace as man learns to consolidate his knowledge and apply it in mastering his environment.

Leadership is an exciting task for the person who understands that his role is the most responsible of all human tasks, for without leaders there are no organizations, and without organizations society is chaos. He who would fulfill his own ego ideal as an executive must seek the excitement of the horizons or he will be dulled by the grinding burden of responsibility which he cannot adequately discharge. Life is too short for that. To seek new stimulation in the more gratifying use of oneself is to live with anticipation of continued self-satisfaction. That anticipation is an experience to which every person is entitled. Giving up the Great Jackass Fallacy is an important way of attaining it.